DIFFERENT STAGES THROUGH THE AGES

Student Manual

DEVELOPED BY
EDUCATION DEVELOPMENT CENTER, INC.

KENDALL/HUNT PUBLISHING COMPANY
4050 Westmark Drive   P.O. Box 1840   Dubuque, Iowa 52004-1840

This book was prepared with the support of National Science Foundation (NSF) Grant ESI-9255722. However, any opinions, findings, conclusions and/or recommendations herein are those of the author and do not necessarily reflect the view of NSF.

Library of Congress Catalog Card Number: 96-80277

ISBN 0-7872-2208-9

Printed in the United States of America

10   9   8   7   6   5   4   3   2   1

EDC Education Development Center, Inc.

CENTER FOR SCIENCE EDUCATION

Dear Students:

Welcome to *Insights in Biology*. This module, *Different Stages Through the Ages*, explores the changes that occur in organisms over the course of their lives and examines one of life's greatest mysteries: the development of a complex, multicellular organism from a single cell. You will follow the growth and development of organisms as they move through the various stages of their lives and examine the biological mechanisms which regulate these changes. You will also investigate external factors which may interfere with the ordered and sequential progression of these events and alter the structure and/or functions in the organism.

Glance through the pages of this manual. Your first instinct is correct: This is not a traditional biology textbook. Although textbooks provide a good deal of useful information, they are not the only way to discover science. In this Student Manual, you will find that chapters have been replaced by Learning Experiences that include readings and activities. The activities include laboratory experimentation, role playing, concept mapping, model building, simulation exercises, and a research project. These learning experiences emphasize the processes of science and the connections among biological concepts.

One of our main goals is to engage you in the excitement of biology. The study of biology is much more than facts. It is a discipline that is as alive as the subjects it portrays: new questions arise, new theories are proposed, and new understandings are achieved. As a result of these new insights, technologies are developed which will impact your everyday lives and the kinds of decisions you will need to make. We hope that this curriculum encourages you to ask questions, to develop greater problem-solving and thinking skills, and to recognize the importance of science in your life.

Insights in Biology Staff

55 CHAPEL STREET
NEWTON, MASSACHUSETTS 02158-1060
TELEPHONE: 617-969-7100
FAX: 617-630-8439

TABLE OF CONTENTS

LEARNING EXPERIENCES

APPENDIX

Those Terrible Blue Tablets

PROLOGUE The changes that organisms undergo—that is, their *development,* as they move through life from single cell to aged adult—have been described as one of life's greatest mysteries. It has been the source of wonder throughout human history. Philosophers, artists, theologians, poets, writers, and scientists have all attempted in their own ways to describe and explain this commonplace, yet amazing, phenomenon. Scientific research has only begun to uncover the biological processes that occur during this highly organized series of events which occur in a predictable and tightly controlled sequence; and yet, even if the entire biology of the process, right down to the last gene and molecule, were dissected, understood and explained, the phenomenon of development of a multicellular organism would remain a source of wonder and inspiration.

You have seen and experienced many developmental changes already in your life. How are you different now from when you were just born? What changes occurred as you became a toddler? a school-aged child? a teenager? How might these changes occur? What do you think controls these changes?

The Sleeping Pill Babies

READING

In the early 1960s, a mysterious outbreak of a condition called *phocomelia* (from the Greek *phoke*, meaning seal, and *melos*, meaning limb) appeared in newborn infants. First in Germany, then in Britain, Canada, and Australia, many infants were born with grossly deformed limbs; arms so short that their hands extended almost directly from their shoulders; legs which failed to grow normally, causing their toes to protrude from their hips; a strawberry birthmark which extended from the forehead across the nose to the upper lip. Many babies had heart defects and deformed intestines. What caused these deformities? Was it something in the environment or something their mothers did or did not do? If so, why did it affect only the developing embryo and not the mother?

Thalidomide
ACCOUNT OF DRIVE TO UNMASK DRUG READS LIKE DETECTIVE STORY

By William L. Laurence, New York Times, August 5, 1962.

The terrible price paid by several thousand babies born with only rudimentary arms and legs to expectant mothers in West Germany who took the new synthetic drug, thalidomide, as a sleeping pill or tranquilizer, serves as a tragic reminder of the fact, hitherto largely disregarded, that a drug that appears to be otherwise relatively safe may inflict terrible damage on the embryo when taken by the mother during the critical stages of the embryo's development.

The tragedy of the "sleeping pill babies" may, on further studies of the manner in which thalidomide produces deformities of the limbs and other serious side-effects, shed new light on the causes of congenital malformations, at present largely a mystery. It may also lead to a re-examination of the question of whether a pregnant woman should take any drug—unless its use is prescribed by a qualified physician.

The disastrous results of thalidomide were described by Dr. Helen B. Taussig, Professor of Pediatrics at the Johns Hopkins School of Medicine, who made a thorough study of the subject, as the "most extraordinary and terrifying experience of our day and age." Professor Taussig, with Dr. Alfred Blalock, a Johns Hopkins surgeon, conceived the famous "blue baby" operation, a life-saving procedure for babies born with a defective circulation.

FIRST WARNING

It was Dr. Taussig who first warned American physicians, at a meeting of the American College of Physicians last April, of the dangers of thalidomide to unborn babies. She tells further details of the gruesome story, one of the most dramatic detective stories of modern medicine, in two articles, one in the June 30 [1962] issue of the American Medical Association and another in the current number of the Scientific American.

The deformities traced to thalidomide are a malformation known as phocomelia, or "seal limb," from the Greek words phoke, meaning seal, and melos, meaning limb. The disease is so rare that most physicians never see it in a lifetime. German physicians therefore were puzzled to explain a mysterious increase in the number of cases of phocomelia.

Figure 1.1
Child with phocomelia ("seal limbs").

INFANT DEFORMITIES

First reports of two grossly deformed infants were presented at an exhibit at a meeting of the pediatricians of the Federal Republic of Germany in October, 1960, in Kassel. Photographs and X-ray pictures—presented by Drs. W. Kosenow and R. A. Pfeiffer of the Institute of Human Genetics in Muenster—showed that the long bones of the infants' arms had almost completely failed to grow; their arms were so short that their hands extended almost directly from their shoulders. Their legs were less affected but showed signs of similar distortion of growth.

During 1961, the incidence of phocomelia increased rapidly, hundreds of afflicted babies being born. At a meeting of German pediatricians in Duesseldorf in November, 1961, almost all had become aware of the mysterious outbreak of phocomelia. At that meeting, Dr. Widikind Lenz of Hamburg University, the Sherlock Holmes of the story, made the disclosure that he tentatively traced the disease to a new drug that had come into use in sedative and sleeping tablets. He did not mention this drug by name, but he told the meeting that it had been marketed in Germany "as freely as aspirin" from 1959 into the spring of 1961. Dr. Lenz' suspicions were aroused after he noticed that about 20 per cent of the mothers questioned reported having taken the drug. He then sent out a second questionnaire in which he specifically asked about the drug, and 50 per cent reported its use.

COMPILING EVIDENCE

On the evening of November 20, 1961, Dr. Lenz announced at the meeting his suspicion of the unnamed drug as the cause of the phocomelia spread, and he also reported that he had urged its German manufacturer to withdraw it from sale. That night a physician came up to Dr. Lenz and said: "Will you tell me confidentially, is the drug Contergan (the German trade name for thalidomide)? I ask because we have such a child and my wife took Contergan." Before the meeting was over, the doctors generally knew that Lenz suspected Contergan. On Nov. 26 the manufacturer of thalidomide—Chemie Gruenenthal—withdrew the drug and all compounds containing it from the market.

Continuing his sleuthing, Dr. Lenz set out to investigate the exact connection between phocomelia and the drug and to fix reliably the date or dates of exposure to the drug in each case. By the middle of March of this year he had compiled fifty case histories in which he had established documentary evidence for use of the drug and had determined the dates of the last menstrual period before pregnancy. He had proof in each case of the date or dates on which thalidomide was taken.

All but five of the women, he determined, had taken the drug between the thirtieth and fiftieth day after the last menstrual period, and the five had taken it between the fiftieth and sixtieth day. In the twenty-one instances in which Dr. Lenz managed to ascertain the date of conception, the mother had taken the drug between the twenty-eighth and the forty-second day after conception.

OTHER CAUSES SUSPECTED

In the human embryo the first signs of future limbs can be discerned with a microscope when the embryo is only ten days old, Dr. Taussig writes in the Scientific American. By 42 days, the tiny limbs are visible to the naked eye although the embryo is only a little more than an inch long.

"The fact that the arm buds develop slightly earlier than those of the legs," Dr. Taussig states, "may be of significance in accounting for the greater frequency of arm damage. As the malformations indicate, the drug arrests and deranges these processes of development that are in progress when the embryo is exposed to it."

EPILOGUE

Despite the devastating effects on developing embryos, thalidomide is making a comeback. Researchers and physicians are examining this drug as a source of relief from many different diseases. Thalidomide has been shown to be effective in clearing up skin lesions in patients with Hansen's Disease (leprosy), in treating mouth ulcerations and in reversing the debilitating weight loss in AIDS patients, in relieving the symptoms of rheumatoid arthritis, in preventing age-related macular degeneration and diabetic retinopathy (blindness), and in halting the growth and spread of tumors. How is it possible that the drug scourge of the 1960s is being viewed by some as the wonder drug of the 1990s?

▶ ANALYSIS

Write responses to the following in your notebook.

1. From your own experience and the discussion in the previous class session, list and describe the stages that humans go through during their lifetimes.

2. What differences might exist between the embryonic and adult stages of a human that would account for the difference in the way thalidomide affects each?

3. Medical practitioners warn pregnant women (or even women of childbearing age who may be trying to become pregnant) not to take certain substances into their bodies. Name three of these substances and describe for each why you think this warning is given.

4. What kinds of information might investigators have needed to know to determine that thalidomide was the cause of the birth defects? How might they have proven the connection experimentally?

ACTIVITY ▶

You Must Have Been a Beautiful Seedling

INTRODUCTION   In different organisms, the major developmental stages have specific names. For example, a fly which undergoes a complete physical change begins life as a fertilized egg, develops into a larval form called a maggot, undergoes a pupal stage and emerges as an adult fly. In this activity, you will be comparing human developmental stages to those of other organisms. Do all organisms develop? How closely do the stages of other organisms correlate to the human stages of development?

▶ TASK

Below are the different stages of four organisms. The stages are not given in the order in which they occur during the organism's lifetime. Place the stages in the developmental order as they compare to human stages. Make a table in your notebook with the four human stages (which you identified in class) on the left. Fill in the table by placing the comparable stages of each of the four organisms seen in Figure 1.2. You may use resources such as a dictionary, encyclopedia, or textbook references.

Figure 1.2
Which comes first?

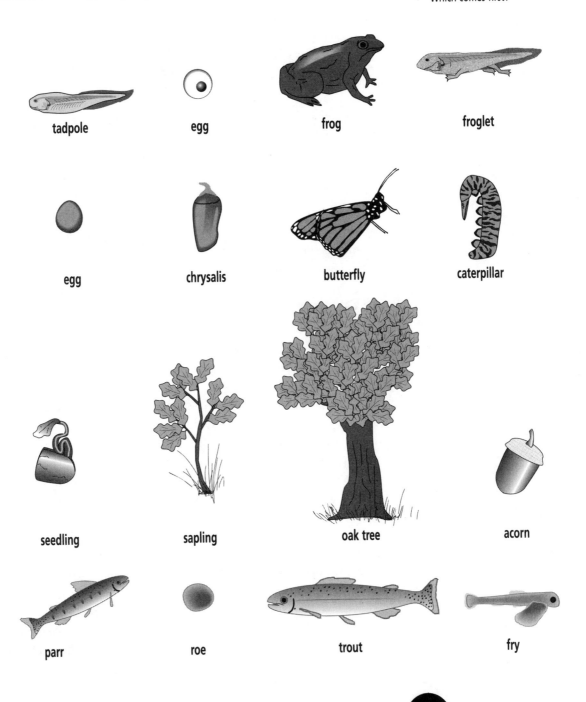

tadpole   egg   frog   froglet

egg   chrysalis   butterfly   caterpillar

seedling   sapling   oak tree   acorn

parr   roe   trout   fry

► ANALYSIS

When you have completed the table, write responses to the following in your notebook.

1. Explain your reasoning for placing the developmental stages of each organism where you did on the table.

2. What do you notice about the sequence of the different stages?

3. In which stages do you think the most changes occur? Explain your answer.

EXTENDING IDEAS

▶ The Food and Drug Administration is responsible for testing and determining the efficacy as well as the possible side effects of different pharmaceuticals being developed by companies in this country. Research how this department of the government goes about determining which drugs should be made available to the public.

▶ The March of Dimes is an organization dedicated to the prevention of birth defects. Contact your local chapter and find out what recommendations they make to pregnant women in order to protect their developing embryos.

IN THE JOB

PHARMACIST   Do you wonder exactly how the chemical compounds in medicines and drugs interact with both healthy and sick people? Pharmacists use their knowledge of chemical compounds and their properties to help develop new drugs or find new uses for old ones, prepare and dispense drugs, inform the general public about how to properly use medications, keep records of the medicines prescribed to individuals and advise of any potential side effects of drug interactions. Most pharmacists practice in community pharmacies, but many others practice in hospitals, other types of health care facilities, a branch of the government or in the pharmaceutical industry. Pharmacists who are employed in the pharmaceutical industry may be involved in research to help develop new drugs, in supervising the preparation of ingredients which medications are made of, including testing raw materials to ensure consistency or in advertising or marketing a company's products. Pharmacists have a minimum of a bachelor's degree in pharmacy (five years post-high school study). A degree from a pharmacy college is required, but one to two years of post-high school study can be in a junior or undergraduate college. Also, pharmacists must take a state licensing exam and complete a one-year internship. Pharmacists interested in research should have a master's or doctorate in pharmacy. Classes such as mathematics, chemistry, biology, computer courses and English are recommended.

PACKAGING OPERATOR   A packaging operator uses manual and/or automated packaging systems to label, inspect, and package final drug containers. He or she also enters data and imprints computer-generated labels, maintains records, and maintains the manufacturing/production area to comply with regulatory requirements, good manufacturing practices, and standard operating procedures. A packaging operator may also perform initial checks of completed documents for completeness and accuracy. The position requires a high school diploma or equivalent and a minimum of 0 to 2 years' experience in a manufacturing environment.

TAKING A LONG, CAREFUL LOOK

PROLOGUE Sprouting from a seed, the roots of a new bean plant carve into the earth, branching out and collecting minerals and water. Tiny leaves unfold and begin to grow and develop in order to use the light from the sun and carbon dioxide from the air to make food that the growing plant requires. A tadpole begins to undergo metamorphosis; tiny jumping legs and forearms appear as its tail begins to recede. These limbs grow in size and strength as the metamorphosis to adult frog is achieved. Clinging to its mother's pouch, a young kangaroo takes in nutrients and completes the growth and development that will enable it to survive independently. A human hand in a developing fetus changes from a paddle shape to a remarkably complex set of fingers. Later, parents watch their young infants use these fingers to pick up toys, to write words, and ultimately, to attain the great dexterity needed for such tasks as playing a musical instrument or using a computer.

All organisms in the plant and animal world undergo growth and development during their lifetimes. These changes, while unique to each organism, demonstrate many similarities. How do we know what changes occur over time in organisms? Understandings about the processes of life have been achieved by making careful observations, asking questions about these observations, forming hypotheses, and finding explanations through experimentation or further observation. Investigating the growth and development that occur during the lifetime of an organism requires careful observation and data collection. In this learning experience, you begin a long-term project in which you will observe the growth and development of several different organisms over time. Throughout the course of the module you will observe these organisms, keep records of the changes that the organisms are undergoing, and apply new concepts about growth and development in interpreting your observations.

Take This Fish and Look at It

by Scudder, Samuel H. from Readings for Writers, *Jo Ray McCuen and Anthony C. Winkler, eds., Harcourt Brace Jovanovich, San Diego, 1974, pp. 201–205.*

Samuel H. Scudder (1837–1911), an American scientist who was educated at Williams College and Harvard University, was one of the most learned and productive entomologists of his day. His main scientific contributions were in the study of butterflies and Orthoptera (an order of insects that includes grasshoppers and crickets).

Scudder realized the primary importance of very careful observation in working with insects. Most of us tend to look at things without really seeing what is there. In everyday life this lack of observation may not be noticed, but in science it is a serious failing. At Harvard Scudder had been a student of Louis Agassiz (1807–1873), the distinguished natural history professor who subjected his students to a rigorous but useful exercise in observation. The following is Scudder's account of one such exercise.

It was more than fifteen years ago that I entered the laboratory of Professor Agassiz, and told him I had enrolled my name in the Scientific School as a student of natural history. He asked me a few questions about my object in coming, my antecedents generally, the mode in which I afterwards proposed to use the knowledge I might acquire, and, finally, whether I wished to study any special branch. To the latter I replied that, while I wished to be well grounded in all departments of zoology, I purposed to devote myself specially to insects.

"When do you wish to begin?" he asked.

"Now," I replied.

This seemed to please him, and with an energetic "Very well!" he reached from a shelf a huge jar of specimens in yellow alcohol. "Take this fish," he said, "and look at it; we call it a haemulon; by and by I will ask what you have seen."

With that he left me, but in a moment returned with explicit instructions as to the care of the object entrusted to me.

"No man is fit to be a naturalist," said he, "who does not know how to take care of specimens."

I was to keep the fish before me in a tin tray, and occasionally moisten the surface with alcohol from the jar, always taking care to replace the stopper tightly. Those were not the days of ground-glass stoppers and elegantly shaped exhibition jars; all the old students will recall the huge neckless glass bottles with their leaky, wax-besmeared corks, half eaten by insects, and begrimed with cellar dust. Entomology was a cleaner science than ichthyology, but the example of the

Professor, who had unhesitatingly plunged to the bottom of the jar to produce the fish, was infectious; and though this alcohol had a "very ancient and fish-like smell," I really dared not show any aversion within these sacred precincts, and treated the alcohol as though it were pure water. Still I was conscious of a passing feeling of disappointment, for gazing at a fish did not commend itself to an ardent entomologist. My friends at home, too, were annoyed when they discovered that no amount of eau-de-Cologne would drown the perfume which haunted me like a shadow.

In ten minutes I had seen all that could be seen in that fish, and started in search of the Professor—who had, however, left the Museum; and when I returned, after lingering over some of the odd animals stored in the upper apartment, my specimen was dry all over. I dashed the fluid over the fish as if to resuscitate the beast from a fainting fit, and looked with anxiety for a return of the normal sloppy appearance. This little excitement over, nothing was to be done but to return to a steadfast gaze at my mute companion. Half an hour passed—an hour—another hour; the fish began to look loathsome. I turned it over and around; looked it in the face—ghastly; from behind, beneath, above, sideways, at a three-quarters' view—just as ghastly. I was in despair; at an early hour I concluded that lunch was necessary; so, with infinite relief, the fish was carefully replaced in the jar, and for an hour I was free.

On my return, I learned that Professor Agassiz had been at the Museum, but had gone, and would not return for several hours. My fellow students were too busy to be disturbed by continued conversation. Slowly I drew forth that hideous fish, and with a feeling of desperation again looked at it. I might not use a magnifying-glass; instruments of all kinds were interdicted. My two hands, my two eyes, and the fish: it seemed a most limited field. I pushed my finger down its throat to feel how sharp the teeth were. I began to count the scales in the different rows, until I was convinced that that was nonsense. At last a happy thought struck me—I would draw the fish; and now with surprise I began to discover new features in the creature. Just then the Professor returned.

"That is right," said he; "a pencil is one of the best of eyes. I am glad to notice, too, that you keep your specimen wet, and your bottle corked."

With these encouraging words, he added:

"Well, what is it like?"

He listened attentively to my brief rehearsal of the structure of parts whose names were still unknown to me: the fringed gill-arches and movable operculum; the pores of the head, fleshy lips and lidless eyes; the lateral line, the spinous fins and forked tail; the compressed and arched body. When I finished, he waited as if expecting more, and then, with an air of disappointment:

"You have not looked very carefully; why," he continued more earnestly, "you haven't even seen one of the most conspicuous features of the animal, which is plainly before your eyes as the fish itself; look again, look again!" and he left me to my misery.

I was piqued; I was mortified. Still more of that wretched fish! But now I set myself to my task with a will, and discovered one new thing after another, until I saw how just the Professor's criticism had been. The afternoon passed quickly; and when, towards its close, the Professor inquired:

"Do you see it yet?"

"No," I replied, "I am certain I do not, but I see how little I saw before."

"That is next best," said he, earnestly, "but I won't hear you now; put away your fish and go home; perhaps you will be ready with a better answer in the morning. I will examine you before you look at the fish."

This was disconcerting. Not only must I think of my fish all night, studying, without the object before me, what this unknown but most visible feature might be; but also, without reviewing my discoveries, I must give an exact account of them the next day. I had a bad memory; so I walked home by Charles River in a distracted state, with my two perplexities.

The cordial greeting from the Professor the next morning was reassuring; here was a man who seemed to be quite as anxious as I that I should see for myself what he saw.

"Do you perhaps mean," I asked, "that the fish has symmetrical sides with paired organs?"

His thoroughly pleased "Of course! Of course!" repaid the wakeful hours of the previous night. After he had discoursed most happily and enthusiastically—as he always did—upon the importance of this point, I ventured to ask what I should do next.

"Oh, look at your fish!" he said, and left me again to my own devices. In a little more than an hour he returned, and heard my new catalogue.

"That is good, that is good!" he repeated; "but that is not all; go on;" and so for three long days he placed that fish before my eyes, forbidding me to look at anything else, or to use any artificial aid. "Look, look, look," was his repeated injunction.

This was the best entomological lesson I ever had—a lesson whose influence has extended to the details of every subsequent study; a legacy the Professor had left to me, as he has left it to so many others, of inestimable value, which we could not buy, with which we cannot part.

A year afterward, some of us were amusing ourselves with chalking outlandish beasts on the Museum blackboard. We drew prancing starfishes; frogs in mortal combat; hydra-headed worms; stately crawfishes, standing on their tails, bearing aloft umbrellas; and grotesque fishes with gaping mouths and staring eyes. The Professor came in shortly after, and was as amused as any at our experiments. He looked at the fishes.

"Haemulons, every one of them," he said; "Mr. _____ drew them."

True; and to this day, if I attempt a fish, I can draw nothing but haemulons.

The fourth day, a second fish of the same group was placed beside the first, and I was bidden to point out the resemblances and differences between the two; another and another followed, until the entire family lay before me, and a whole legion of jars covered the table and surrounding shelves; the odor had become a pleasant perfume; and even now, the sight of an old, six-inch, worm-eaten cork brings fragrant memories.

The whole group of haemulons was thus brought in review; and, whether engaged upon the dissection of the internal organs, the preparation and examination of the bony framework, or the description of the various parts, Agassiz's training in the method of observing facts and their orderly arrangement was ever accompanied by the urgent exhortation not to be content with them.

"Facts are stupid things," he would say, "until brought into connection with some general law."

At the end of eight months, it was almost with reluctance that I left these friends and turned to insects; but what I had gained by this outside experience has been of greater value than years of later investigation in my favorite groups.

▶ ANALYSIS

Write brief responses to the following in your notebook.

1. Why do you think Samuel Scudder wasn't allowed to use any equipment to observe the fish?

2. What do you think Professor Agassiz meant when he said that a pencil is one of the best eyes?

3. In what ways were Scudder's later observations different from his earlier observations? What does this tell you about observing, and about what it means to observe closely?

4. In class you discussed the difference between looking and observing. Elaborate on ideas about this difference based on this reading.

PEANUT, PEANUT, WHERE'S MY PEANUT?

INTRODUCTION   "Most of us tend to look at things without really seeing what is there. In everyday life this lack of observation may not be noticed, but in science it is a serious failing." This statement highlights the difference between just looking and observing. Why are careful observation and data collection important? You may have measured growth and observed physical changes in plant studies, or made observations of chemical reactions. In order to understand *how* an event occurs, you must observe *what* is happening. In this activity, you will be looking at a peanut in order to develop two important skills of science: observation and communication. You will be relying on these skills throughout the rest of the module.

▶ MATERIALS NEEDED

For each group of eight students:
- 1 paper bag containing 10 peanuts
- 8 index cards (3 inch x 5 inch)

▶ PROCEDURE

1. Have someone from your group collect the materials for the activity. Hand out one index card to each group member.

2. Remove one peanut from the bag and examine it closely for one minute.

3. Return your peanut to the bag. When all the peanuts have been returned to the bag, shake it to mix the peanuts.

4. Pour the contents onto a table or flat surface. Try to pick out your peanut.

5. Return all the peanuts to the bag and shake it again.

6. Take a new peanut and examine it closely for one minute.

7. Write a complete description of this peanut on the index card.

8. Return your peanut to the bag.

9. Pass your index card to the person on your left and take the index card from the person on your right.

10. Shake the bag and again pour its contents onto a table or flat surface.

11. Try to pick out the peanut described on the index card you are now holding. When your group has finished, determine whether your identification was successful by asking the person from whom you received the card.

▶ ANALYSIS

Write responses to the following questions in your notebook.

1. Were you successful in identifying the first peanut? Why or why not?

2. Were you successful in identifying the second peanut? If yes, what "peanut characteristics" enabled you to do so? If not, what further observational information did you need?

BEGINNING AT THE BEGINNING

INTRODUCTION   You are about to embark on a long-term study of how organisms change over time. For this project you will need to use several skills which include:

* *patience*—the organisms will change over time but the observations require a certain amount of patience; the organisms that have been selected for study were chosen in part because of their more rapid development time

* *observation*—as has been practiced and discussed in class, observation skills are critical in exploring growth and development; patience and careful observation will reward you with some remarkable insights into the changes the organisms are undergoing

* *data collection*—careful and accurate data collection is essential for keeping good records; remember that you cannot go back and look again; time marches on for all organisms and once the moment of growth, development, and change has occurred it can never be recaptured with that particular individual organism

* *communication*—sharing your observations accurately and completely with your group will be very important; each member of your group is responsible for observing and analyzing all of the different kinds of organisms and each must be able to rely on someone else's observations; in addition, clear communication to another member of your group will assist each member in understanding your perspectives and ideas and to contribute more meaningfully to group discussion and analysis

* *analysis*—as your organisms mature, you will apply the concepts from the module to describe and interpret patterns of growth and development

The members of your group will be setting up a habitat for one type of organism and maintaining these organisms—feeding them, ensuring that their environment is clean, at the correct temperature, and disturbed as little as necessary. Each member of the class will be responsible for comparing the growth and development of your group's organism to all the other organisms in the class. Each kind of organism to be observed has been selected as a good representative of one or more of the stages of development that you discussed at the beginning of this learning experience.

You will want to determine how best to make these observations and how to divide the work within the group in order to be sure that data collection is complete for all the organisms and shared by all in the group. The success of this long-term project will depend on your skills in observation, in recording the observations that you make, in applying the concepts from the module, and in sharing them with the rest of your group.

The following investigation will help you begin to practice some of these skills in preparation for your work on the long-term project.

▶ MATERIALS NEEDED

For each group of four students:
- 1 specimen sample (egg, larva, or seed)
- 4 hand lenses
- 1 ruler
- 4 index cards (3 inch x 5 inch)

▶ PROCEDURE

1. Obtain a specimen of the organism that your group will be maintaining for the long-term project. This will be either an egg, a seed, or a larva. Have one member of your group gather the remaining materials.

2. Using your own ideas as well as those from the class discussion, list in your notebook what features or characteristics of your specimen that you plan to observe.

3. Take turns looking carefully at your specimen with and without the hand lens. Draw and describe in your notebook what you see in as much detail as possible.

4. Obtain four blank index cards and give one to each group member. Write a name or number to designate your group on a corner of each card.

5. On your index card, write down one observation you made while examining the specimen.

6. Have one student in your group collect the four cards, shuffle them, and pass one card back to each student.

7. First observations are usually simple. Write a comment about the observation you received that would make it more meaningful and useful. Remarks might include:
   – what else you need to know
   – posing questions you may have
   – contradictions you observed
   – supporting observations you made

8. When you have written a comment or a response on the card, pass this card to the group member on your left, so that everyone has a new card. Then comment on what is on the new card in front of you. Continue this process until each group member has responded to each card.

9. At the end of class, hand in all index cards to the teacher; they will be returned for discussion in the next session.

NOTE: Even if you receive your own card back, you should still write a comment. It can be helpful to think more about your own ideas as well as those of others.

▶ ANALYSIS

Write responses to the following in your notebook.

1. Using the list of all the organisms that will be used in the long-term project, write a short but detailed description of what you predict will happen to each type of organism as you observe it over the course of the project. You may use words, diagrams, or labeled drawings in your descriptions.

2. Obtain your group's four index cards. Read the comments on the cards and analyze the information from the comments about the specimen. What is the importance of the information added by each student?

3. Do your observations give you any indication about how your organism might change as it develops? If so, how?

4. What questions came to mind as you examined your organism? Did the other observations or comments answer your questions? If not, how might you answer them during the project?

NOTE: If your group's observations and comments on the cards did not answer all the questions, speculate about what is missing from the comments, and about what additional observations you might need that would help you answer those questions.

WHAT IS A LONG-TERM PROJECT, ANYWAY?

INTRODUCTION   What changes occur as a seemingly lifeless fish egg floating in water becomes a swimming creature? Do similar changes occur in an egg no bigger than a speck of dust as it develops into an insect? This long-term project will enable you to address these questions and others that will arise during the weeks to come. During this learning experience you have been developing your observation and communication skills. For the remainder of the module you will use those skills as you make observations, ask questions, share your observations with your group, and analyze the growth and development of different types of organisms.

You will begin the project using organisms in the early stage of their life cycles—eggs, seeds, or larvae. Once the organisms have been set up in their habitats you will observe them regularly.

At the end of the project you will be responsible for writing up the results of your observations in a report in which you will describe the developmental events that occurred for each organism and compare these events among the different organisms.

▶ MATERIALS NEEDED

For each group of four students:
- access to a compound or dissecting microscope
- 4 copies of Information Pages (for one organism)
- 4 project laboratory notebooks for recording observations, questions, ideas
- 1 thermometer (optional)
- 4 hand lenses
- 1 ruler
- 1 set of materials for care and maintenance of the organism

▶ PROCEDURE

1. Before beginning your study, make sure to read all the Information Pages about the growth and habitat requirements of your group's organism.

2. Set up your project laboratory notebook, which will serve as your own, ongoing record of your project. You will record all information pertinent to your study in this notebook as the organisms grow and develop. As in a research laboratory, original notes are entered in the notebook as an integral part of research. The notebook acts as a place to record your data and to write down questions, comments, and ideas that will help in analyzing your results. This data will be part of your final project report. Therefore, the notebook should remain in class with the project so as not to lose original notes. You may wish to divide the notebook into sections, one section for each type of specimen. All entries into the notebook must be dated.

Begin the setup of your laboratory notebook with the following information:

- statistics about your group
  - members' names
  - homerooms
  - daily class schedules
  - home telephone numbers (Your group members may want to contact each other if anyone observes the organisms during non-class time and something exciting is happening.)
- the name of the organism being studied
- a diagram and description of the habitat you set up for the organisms, including
  - temperature
  - light conditions
  - volume of water, if applicable
  - type and amount of food, if applicable
  - any other data that may be significant

3. Determine with your group members what kinds of information you will be collecting, how you will collect it, and how you will record it. You should agree upon the following:

- the kind of measurements you should make
- other variables to observe, such as color, patterns, and changes in structures or form
- the way in which you will record measurements and observations
- a schedule for each group member, for taking turns collecting data

4. In addition to observing your own organism, you will be responsible for comparing the growth and development of your organism to the other organisms being maintained by other groups. If there are a lot of different organisms, you will need to determine what kind of data (such as drawings, measurements, etc.) to collect, and how to communicate with each other about these observations. Each group member will be responsible for one other organism in addition to the group's organism. This member will be responsible for making observations and collecting measurements and data about the organism to share with the rest of the group.

5. Each member of the group should read and take notes on the Background and Life Cycle information posted near the habitats of the organisms.

6. At the end of the project you will write up your results and conclusions in a final laboratory report. Each student will write an individ-

ual report, based on the data collected by the group and on any conversations with other groups. The following is to be included in your report:

- project title

- names of research group members

- brief description of the organism's habitat

- methods used to take measurements and collect data on your group's organism and on other organisms

- data clearly presented including graphs where appropriate (Include a series of diagrams of your group's organism depicting changes observed over time. Data must also include at least one labeled diagram for each of the other organisms.)

- a comparison of developmental stages among the different organisms observed, including similarities and differences in the patterns of development

- analysis in which the link between concepts in the module and your observations of all the organisms are clearly presented

- sources of error which may have occurred

- new questions arising out of these observations, and at least three suggestions for further study

7. At the end of the project, after you have written the laboratory report, your group will present your findings and conclusions to the class. The following is to be included in the presentation:

- experimental set-up

- relevant observations and other data on your organism

- analysis of and understandings derived from your data

- conclusions stating the major factors of your organism's developmental process

- comparison with other organisms observed

- general conclusions of organismal developmental processes

- drawings and diagrams

EXTENDING IDEAS

ON THE JOB

FISHERY BIOLOGIST   Are you fascinated by fish? Fishery biologists are scientists who specialize in the habitats, population dynamics, nutrition, and diseases of fish. Fishery biologists may work to restore species of fish to their natural habitats, manage fish hatcheries for the U.S. Department of Fish and Wildlife, gather data on how environmental changes affect fish populations, propagate species of fish in hatcheries, and work with other organizations to restore or enhance natural fish habitats. Many fishery biologists are employed with the U.S. Fish and Wildlife Service, an organization committed to conservation and resource management. The Service also offers scientific understanding of fish and their habitats to the public, and offers technical information and advice to other state agencies on fish management. Fishery biologists have a minimum of a four year college degree in biology with some coursework in aquatic subjects and animal sciences to qualify for an entry level position. Advancement is possible with a master's or doctoral degree. Classes such as biology, chemistry, ecology, mathematics, and English are necessary.

ZOOLOGIST   Do you enjoy working with animals and learning about them? Zoologists are scientists who study all aspects of animal life—the anatomy, classification, life histories, habits, growth and development, evolutionary relationships, genetics, distribution, and interactions between an animal and its environment. Usually a zoologist specializes in one class or order of animals, such as fish, insects, or mammals. Zoologists may work in a lab or in the field or both, and employ the laboratory techniques and tools used by ecologists, chemists, geneticists, anatomists, and others. With a four year college degree, positions as laboratory assistants or research assistants are possible. With a master's or doctoral degree, zoologists can teach in a university or pursue independent research in the field. Classes such as biology, chemistry, math, English, and computer science are recommended.

WHICH COMES FIRST, THE CHICKEN OR THE EGG?

PROLOGUE   **W**hat is the starting point for development of a new organism? How does it begin, and what is needed for a whole new organism to "grow"? Development begins in almost every case with a fertilized egg. When most of us think of eggs we simultaneously think toast, juice, and scrambled or sunny side up. But what is an egg, really? An *egg* is a specialized cell produced by females of a species. When it joins or fuses with another kind of cell, a *sperm* produced by the male of the species, it becomes a *fertilized egg* or *zygote*. The egg and sperm are also known as *gametes*.

The *fertilized egg* is yet another kind of cell with a remarkable difference from almost any other cell; it has the potential to become a complete multicellular, complex organism.

A fertilized egg is an entity with incredible potential. Almost every living organism begins life as an egg. This is strikingly illustrated in the frontispiece of William Harvey's *De Generatione Animalium* (Concerning the Generation of Animals) published in 1651, which shows the hand of Jove, a Roman god, holding an egg, or rather an eggshell, out of which has emerged a wide variety of animals: a child, a dolphin, a spider, and so on (see Figure 3.1). Worked into the design is the motto *Ex ova omnia*—everything comes from an egg. As early as 1651, at least some scientists understood the idea that almost everything begins life as an egg.

Figure 3.1
Drawing from Harvey's book, *De Generatione Animalium.*

Gulielmus Harveus de Generatione Animalium.

EGGS-ACTLY

Excerpted from Robert Burton. Eggs: Nature's Perfect Package. *Facts on File, Inc., New York, 1987, pp. 6–9.*

The egg is surely one of nature's most remarkable and versatile inventions. It is a compact, self-contained capsule containing everything necessary for the creation of a new life—be it . . . a moth, an ostrich, or a human being. For millions of years the egg has carried life from one generation to the next, and many ancient civilizations—Egyptians, Indians and Japanese among them—believe that the world itself had been hatched from an egg made by the Creator . . .

The power of the egg's symbolism is enhanced by its beauty of form and colouring. One hundred years ago, the naturalist T. W. Higginson wrote: 'I think if required on pain of death to name the most perfect thing in the universe, I should risk my fate on a bird's egg.' He should not have stopped at a bird's egg; the tiny sculptured button of a butterfly egg and the translucent pearl of a snail egg have their own beauty. But beyond the mystical and aesthetic appreciation of eggs, there is the enormous biological interest of the strategies employed by so many animals in fertilizing, laying and caring for their eggs.

The variety of eggs make their definition far from simple. There is no doubt about the egg on the breakfast table; [had it been fertilized] . . . it might have hatched into a chicken which would have laid more eggs. There is no answer to the old riddle: neither chicken nor egg comes first. They are alternating stages in the never-ending progress of life. . .

The egg is the reproductive unit, produced by the female, which develops into a new individual [when fertilized]. It is a single cell, although very different from the other cells that make up the body. . .

An egg starts as a tiny cell, usually in a specialized organ [of the female]—the ovary. Like other cells it consists essentially of . . . protoplasm enclosed in a membrane and containing a nucleus that holds the genetic material—complex molecules of deoxyribonucleic acid or DNA. These DNA molecules form a blueprint made up of units called genes. Each gene controls one small part of the functioning of the cell and together they determine the structure, physiology and often the behav-

Figure 3.2
In the process of fertilization of a sea urchin egg, a single sperm attaches to the egg (a), penetrates (b), and injects its DNA into the egg (c).

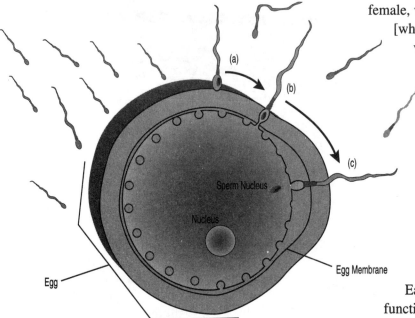

iour of the animal. The nucleus of an egg therefore holds the information needed to build the animal that will develop from it. When the egg is fertilized by a sperm [which contains DNA in its nucleus], their genetic materials meet and mingle, so the zygote (the cell that results from the union of the egg and the sperm) contains a mixture of blueprints from each parent.

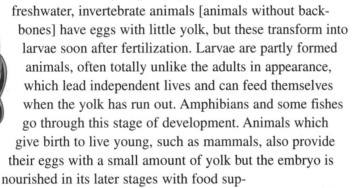

Our ideas of what constitutes an egg are influenced by the circumstances in which the embryo develops from the zygote. All eggs are supplied with yolk to nourish the early growth of the embryo, but further provision must be made for the main period of development when the body is growing. Many marine, and some freshwater, invertebrate animals [animals without backbones] have eggs with little yolk, but these transform into larvae soon after fertilization. Larvae are partly formed animals, often totally unlike the adults in appearance, which lead independent lives and can feed themselves when the yolk has run out. Amphibians and some fishes go through this stage of development. Animals which give birth to live young, such as mammals, also provide their eggs with a small amount of yolk but the embryo is nourished in its later stages with food sup-

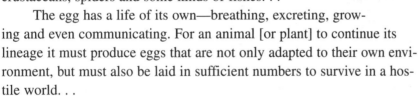

plied by the mother. A third group of animals provides the egg with enough yolk to sustain the embryo through its development. Such eggs are enclosed in a protective shell and are often laid in a nest. These are the eggs of birds, reptiles, insects, crustaceans, spiders and some kinds of fishes. . .

The egg has a life of its own—breathing, excreting, growing and even communicating. For an animal [or plant] to continue its lineage it must produce eggs that are not only adapted to their own environment, but must also be laid in sufficient numbers to survive in a hostile world. . .

Figure 3.3
Examples of eggs.

EPILOGUE

The fertilized egg represents the beginning of life. The design and structure of the egg protects this new stage, the embryonic stage, as it unfolds within. Some eggs, such as a bird's egg, give no indication from the outside of the miraculous events occurring within until the final product emerges. Other eggs lay it out for all to see; the development of the frog from first cleavage to swimming tadpole is visible for anyone who wishes to observe. But regardless of the showmanship of the developing organism, each one is following a blueprint encoded in its DNA, which not only determines what each organism will be, but also what role each cell in the organism will play, how long becoming this organism will take, and ultimately, in many ways how the life of that organism will play out biologically, from beginning (birth, hatching, or germination) to end.

▶ ANALYSIS

Write responses to the following in your notebook.

1. Create a chart in which you define and compare the egg, sperm, and fertilized egg in as many different ways as possible. Use the reading, the list from the class brainstorm, and ideas from the class discussions to help organize the data for your chart.

2. Think of the egg, sperm, and fertilized egg together. How are all three the same? How are they different? Write a paragraph detailing these broader biological similarities and differences.

READING ▶

LIFE'S GREATEST MYSTERY: IDEAS IN HISTORY

Throughout recorded history, humans have pondered the mystery of development and have described their observations and explanations of these observations in their writings and stories.

The following are writings of several individuals who attempted to describe or explain the mystery of new life. As you read the following paragraphs, think about whether you agree with the view presented of the beginning of human life.

An ancient hymn to the sun-god Aton, written by Akhanaton, Amenophis IV, about 1400 B.C. (translated into English by Joseph Needham, Cambridge University Press) describes an Egyptian perspective on embryology:

Creator of the germ in woman,
Maker of the seed in man,
Giving life to the son in the body of his mother,
Soothing him that he may not weep,
Nurse (even) in the womb.
Giver of birth to animate every one that he maketh,
When he cometh forth from the womb on the day of his birth.
Thou openest his mouth in speech,
Thou suppliest his necessity. . .

Among many tribes in Africa and Australia, in some tribes of North American Indians, and at one time widely prevalent in Europe, it was believed that the child emanated from the body of the father and that the mother merely nurtured it. From this belief came the custom of La Couvade which required that the father, at the time of birth, retire to bed as though it were he and not the woman who was delivering the child.

Many early speculations to solve the mystery of birth evolved into mythical explanations, survivals of which are seen in the nursery tales told to children. An old tradition is that the stork brings good luck; an old belief, that the coming of children is good luck. Somehow the two ideas became united—possibly because storks were frequently seen at times of birth, and the superstitious believed that the bird was the good luck omen announcing the infant's arrival.

The Greek philosopher Aristotle (4th century B.C.) argued that the mother contributes the substance and the father the structure of their offspring. Aristotle stated "If, then, the male stands for the effective and active, and the female, considered as female, for the passive, it follows that what the female would contribute to the semen of the male would not be semen but material for the semen to work upon" *(Based on Bekkers Greek text, from* When Did I Begin? Conception of the Human Individual in History, Philosophy and Science *by Norman M. Ford, Cambridge University Press, 1988, p. 26).* He pictured the male's semen as the moving element which organized the substance provided by the female, just as an artist "imparts shape and form to his material." In other words there is a gradual emergence of form from undifferentiated material.

Epicurus (3rd century B.C.) believed that both parents contribute material and that a child must be completely formed from conception, though in miniature. "In the seed are enclosed all the parts of the body of the man that shall be formed. The infant in his mother's womb hath the roots of the beard and hair that he shall wear some day. In the little mass, likewise, are all the lineaments of the body and all that which posterity shall discover in him."

The theory of preformation, popular in the 17th century, stated that the appearance of different organs and parts in the developing fetus was due to the unfolding and growth of parts that already existed in the embryo from the outset. Two forms of preformation appeared. Ovists believed that the whole of the future organism existed within the egg; the sperm merely acted to stimulate the embryo to further development.

Animalculists or spermists believed that the sperm itself already contained a tiny animal (animalcule) fully formed in miniature. In the case of humans this was called the homunculus; this tiny human would begin to grow once in contact with the nurturing environment of the womb (see Figure 3.4).

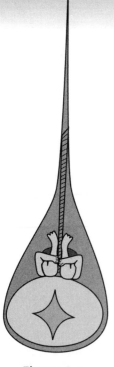

Figure 3.4
Spermists' view of a human sperm.

▶ ANALYSIS

You have just read several descriptions of attempts to explain how new human life is formed. Using whatever format you choose, such as a poem, story, concept map, essay, labeled drawings, etc., explain your own theory of what you think occurs in human growth and development between fertilization and birth. Be sure to include your understandings about the biology of development.

EXTENDING IDEAS

▶ Make an egg collection. Insect eggs are everywhere in the spring and fall, and even in the winter, eggs can be found attached to twigs, branches, trucks, or fence posts. During the warmer months, eggs are readily found on leaf surfaces. A hand lens will help in locating the eggs, but they can also be seen by the naked eye. Insect eggs come in many shapes: milk bottle, barrels, spheres, light bulbs, bullets, flower pots, just to name a few. They may be laid out singly, in rows, in clusters, or on top of each other. They are available in a number of decorative colors. Try to identify each egg you find using field guides and reference books.

Modified from The Practical Entomologist *by Rick Imes, Simon and Schuster, New York, 1992, p. 27*

ON THE JOB

FISH BREEDER Do you find fish fascinating? Would you like to breed them and raise them? Fish breeders often specialize in breeding and raising certain exotic fish such as rare catfish, rare rainbows, African cichlids, fancy guppies, or marine fish which they sell to hobbyists and pet stores. Many breeders also maintain a retail business in selling aquaria, aquarium supplies, and fish food. Some breeders work with fish farms raising fresh water fish such as trout and talapia for consumption. Experience in raising and keeping fish is essential. Courses in biology, oceanography, and business may prove useful.

EMBRYO-GENESIS

PROLOGUE Every living organism, from the tiniest alga to the most enormous whale, develops from a single cell. What changes occur as an organism develops from a single fertilized cell to a multicellular organism with highly specialized structures that enable it to perform the functions necessary to sustain life?

In this and the following three learning experiences, you will be examining *embryogenesis* (the formation and early growth and development of living organisms). During the last 100 years, scientists have shed light on many events of early development; however, much mystery still surrounds the journey from single cell to independent organism.

MY, HOW YOU'VE [NOT] CHANGED

INTRODUCTION Embryonic development can be divided into distinct stages or phases. It is through these phases that the single fertilized egg develops into a complex, multicellular organism. What happens during these phases? Are these phases the same for all multicellular organisms?

In order to respond to these questions, you will examine and compare sequences of embryonic development for several different organisms.

▶ TASK

1. You have been given an envelope containing a series of pictures of embryo development of one organism. Other members of your group have been given pictures of other organisms. Arrange your pictures in the order (sequence) in which you think they occur during embryogenesis.

2. In the classroom, arrange the pictures of your organism on a table or other flat surface, in the order you decided on. Compare the sequence for your organism with the other organisms sequenced by your group.

3. As a group, discuss whether all the sequences appear logical. Make sure there is a group consensus. Then, together, discuss the following Analysis questions in preparation for a class discussion.

▶ ANALYSIS

Write responses to the following in your notebook.

1. How did you decide how to order your pictures?
2. What was the first thing to happen to your organism?
3. Describe what you think is happening in subsequent stages.
4. At what stage were you able to identify specific parts of your organism, such as limbs or the head?
5. At what stage were you able to identify the type (species) of organism? What characteristics helped you identify it as this species?
6. Do you think the development of your organism could occur in some other sequence? Why or why not?
7. What differences and similarities do you notice as you compare the sequences among the different organisms?

READING ▶

BUILDING STABLE FOUNDATIONS

A story is told about the eminent embryologist Karl von Baer. In 1828, he wrote "I have two small embryos preserved in alcohol that I forgot to label. At present I am unable to determine the genus to which they belong. They may be lizards, small birds, or even mammals." The similarities between a four-week-old human embryo and the early embryos of fish, salamanders, turtles, chickens, pigs, sheep, and mice are so striking that it is difficult to tell them apart. What is the biological basis of this? Why do vertebrates start out the same only to become so very different?

Unlike embryos, fully formed organisms show much variation in their physical characteristics. The English naturalist Charles Darwin proposed in his nineteenth-century book *The Origin of Species* that chance variations resulted in some organisms having a particular characteristic which made them better suited for living in their surroundings than others. He further realized that these better-suited individuals are more likely to survive and to leave offspring. This idea, commonly referred to as the "survival of the fittest," is a fundamental principle of evolution.

How is this idea reflected in embryogenesis? The retention of the embryonic pattern of development in so many organisms suggests that this pattern was found in an earlier, common ancestor and was retained because it was a very good foundation from which a variety of organisms could develop.

Embryos develop in an ordered, predictable way; the early sequence of events, in particular, is critical. This embryonic foundation then permits a great diversity of organisms to develop in a similar way. If something goes wrong at this early time, the entire sequence of events can be disrupted, resulting in embryonic death. Differences which can be seen among the different organisms at later stages of development must have been retained by "fit" ancestors, presumably because the new characteristics were beneficial to those ancestors and did not disrupt future stages of development.

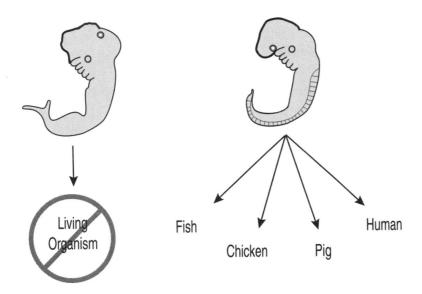

Living Organism

Fish

Chicken

Pig

Human

Figure 4.1
Certain changes in an early embryo may result in embryonic death.

You can think of the "construction" of an organism as you might think of the construction of a house. Foundations for houses have similar requirements and structures; they must be built first so that they can support the rest of the house. On the other hand, the house that is built upon this foundation can vary tremendously in shape. A builder may alter the form of the house in order to please a client. If the change is successful, the house looks different, and others may choose the same form for their house. If the change is not successful, or provides no advantage, it most likely will not be repeated in other buildings. But, whether the next house built looks like the original one or not, it will have a very similar foundation. The foundation shows very little variation even among very different houses.

Similarly, information expressed early in the development of many different organisms most likely is information that has been retained from the DNA of a common ancestor. As an organism begins to develop the characteristics specific to its species, other information in the DNA of the organism is expressed; the information at this stage is specific for this organism and different from that of another species at the same developmental stage. These differences in characteristics are caused by the changes in the information in the DNA over the course of evolution.

Organisms alive today can be viewed as representations of "successful" DNA; these organisms contain and express information in their DNA that has been beneficial and has been passed from generation to generation. Some of it ("*species DNA*") has changed during the course of this passage and has resulted in the different species that we see today. Other DNA contains information that was present in a common ancestor ("*ancestral DNA*") and is inviolate; that is, it cannot be changed without results that are detrimental to the organism. Perhaps this suggests that the embryonic development of vertebrates is the best it can be. On the other hand, it may only mean embryonic development is the way it is because of a particular pathway that was taken during evolution. Another pathway might have worked just as well, but by chance that path was never taken.

▶ ANALYSIS

Write responses to the following in your notebook.

1. Describe, in your own words, why the early embryonic stages of development of different vertebrates resemble each other even though the adult stages look so different. Use your group's sequences of organisms as one reference. Be sure to discuss the differences in the consequences between making changes in structure and function in early embryonic stages versus making changes later on in development.

2. Do you think your DNA still contains information for gills and tails? Why or why not?

3. George Wald, a Nobel Prize awardee, has stated, "The evolution of organisms has left traces in their embryological development." What do you think he meant by this?

READING ▶ FROM SIMPLE BEGINNINGS

Embryogenesis is a series of events which occur in a very specific order. As you examined your pictures you probably observed that development begins with cell division. The single fertilized egg must divide to produce hundreds, thousands, even millions of cells which will eventually make up a fully formed, independently functioning organism. These early stages represent one of the most rapid growth periods in the development of an organism.

After fertilization occurs, the fertilized egg (or zygote) divides into two cells which then continue to divide many, many times, forming a hollow ball of small cells. This ball is called a *blastula*. Cell division occurs so rapidly at this stage that the cells have no time to increase in size. The blastula itself is not much larger than the fertilized egg. Each cell in the blastula contains an entire set of the original zygote DNA.

Within the blastula, the cells begin to move around and arrange themselves in specific patterns. In a process called *gastrulation,* cells organize themselves into a structure of three layers known as the *gastrula.* From these three layers will arise all the structures and organ systems of the organism; the outer layer (*ectoderm*) will become the skin and the nervous system; the middle layer (*mesoderm*) will become the heart and circulatory system, the kidneys, *gonads* (reproductive organs), and connective tissue; and the inner layer (*endoderm*) will become the pancreas, liver, and organs of the digestive system (see Figure 4.2).

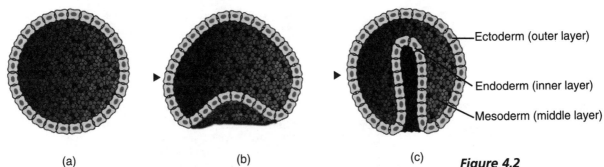

(a)   (b)   (c)

Ectoderm (outer layer)

Endoderm (inner layer)

Mesoderm (middle layer)

Figure 4.2
After blastula formation (a), cells begin to move into position (b), forming three layers (c). These layers will eventually develop into the organs and skeletal structures of the organism.

After gastrulation, the scene is set for the organism to begin to take shape. In Learning Experiences 5, 6, and 7, you will follow these unspecialized cells as they develop specific functions (the process of *differentiation*) and further organize into "working" groups; that is, they begin to associate with cells carrying out similar functions to form tissues, organs and body structures.

During embryogenesis, an organism assumes a specific form— limbs form, a head is shaped, a tail appears (and disappears again later in some cases), and organs form. The embryo is molded and shaped by a series of cell divisions (growth), cell movements, cell associations, and sometimes even by cell death (for instance, the loss of a tail structure or the formation of a human hand and fingers from the paddle shape in the early embryo is the result of the death of cells). As these structures form, the embryo begins to develop functions which will enable it to sustain life; organ systems (for example, the circulatory, nervous, and digestive systems) form (*organogenesis*) and begin to make connections and to function. During the later stages of embryogenesis the functions of the body systems develop further and major growth occurs. Figure 4.3 shows the development from the fertilized egg to organ formation.

For some organisms the form developed during embryogenesis is the form that the organism will maintain throughout its life. For others, it is the first of several shapes the organism will assume. For all multicellular organisms, however, the growth and development begun in the embryo do not cease when the organism reaches the end of the embryonic stage; these activities continue until the beginning of adulthood, and in some cases, well beyond that time.

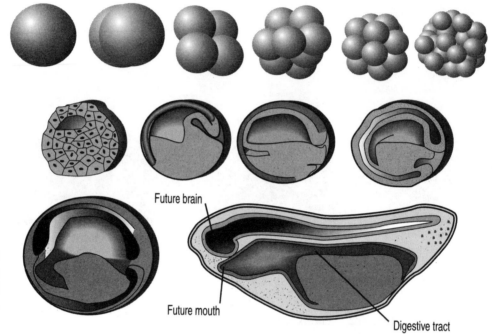

Figure 4.3
Development of an organism from fertilized egg to organ formation.

Future brain

Future mouth

Digestive tract

▶ ANALYSIS

Write responses to the following in your notebook.

1. Lewis Thomas, scientist and essayist, once wrote: "For real amazement, if you wish to be amazed, is this process [embryonic development]. You start out as a single cell derived from the coupling of a sperm and an egg; this divides in two, then four, then eight, and so on. . . The mere existence of such a cell should be one of the great astonishments of the earth. People ought to be walking around all day, all through their waking hours calling to each other in endless wonderment, talking of nothing except that cell."

> *"On Embryology"* © 1979 by Lewis Thomas from The Medusa and the Snail, *used by permission of Viking Penguin, a division of Penguin Books USA, Inc.*

In a paragraph, describe what you think Thomas meant by this. Do you agree or disagree with his sentiment? Explain your response.

2. Describe, in detail, the major events that occur during embryogenesis and explain the significance of these events to the organism's future. You may wish to use Figure 4.3 to help you in your description and explanation.

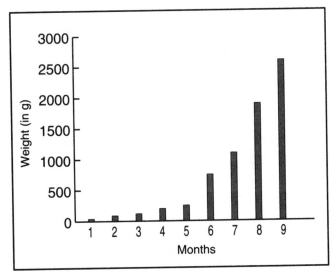

Table 4.4
Increase in weight of embryo during human gestation.

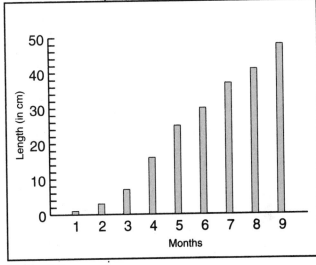

Table 4.5
Increase in length of embryo during human gestation.

3. Tables 4.4 and 4.5 are graphs of the increase in weight and size of a human during *gestation* (human embryogenesis). Using these tables and the readings, describe what you think is happening at both the cellular and organ levels during the different time frames.

4. When is the most important time for an embryo to get nutrients? Why?

EXTENDING IDEAS

▶ The *homology* (similarity in structure) of body parts of different species is often cited as evidence of the descent of vertebrates from a common ancestor. Examine pictures of the bone structure of a human limb, a horse's leg, the wing of a bat, and a whale flipper, then describe similarities and differences in structure and function. Speculate as to how these similarities and differences may have arisen.

▶ Karl von Baer, a great embryologist of the early nineteenth century, once remarked that gastrulation is the most important event in anyone's life—more important than birth, graduation, and marriage. Explain why you think he said this.

▶ Research different drugs that can affect the developing embryo. Determine the period of the embryo's greatest sensitivity, and how the drug may alter its development.

▮❶N THE JOB

EVOLUTIONARY BIOLOGIST   Are you interested in using clues from the past to explain ideas of the present? Evolutionary biologists study the growth and change of organisms over time and examine their relatedness to one another. Some evolutionary biologists use the tools of cellular, genetic, or molecular biology to look at DNA sequences among different organisms and determine how they have changed over time. Other evolutionary biologists look at the morphology of organisms or their skeletal structures to compare structure and function. When they look at fossil animals and plants, they may use the tools of paleontologists, including knowledge of geology, or those of anatomists. Most evolutionary biologists conduct their research in affiliation with a university and have doctoral degrees. Classes such as biology, chemistry, geology, history of science, math, English, and computer science are useful.

Playing Your Position

PROLOGUE   How does a developing organism change from a ball of cells into a complex, multicellular organism with specialized parts and functions? What ensures that a head develops where it belongs, and all the systems of the body have all the right parts in all the right places?

The early stages of embryogenesis set the developing embryo on an organized and sequential course. Cells begin to express specialized functions and become part of the organism's structures and organ systems. During this period the destinies of each cell and its descendants are determined. In this learning experience, you will use models to explore the importance of a cell's location and communication with other cells in determining what it will become in the developing embryo.

Is It Fate?

Imagine that your teacher lined up every member of your class in four groups and announced that everyone in group 1 would become a construction worker, everyone in group 2 would become an administrative assistant, everyone in group 3 would become a doctor, and everyone in group 4 would become a teacher. Your fate, so to speak, would be determined by your position in the lineup. In addition, not only would your own professional future be determined by this position, but so would that of your children; you as a teacher could only beget teachers.

GROUP 1—CONSTRUCTION WORKERS

GROUP 2—ADMINISTRATIVE ASSISTANTS

GROUP 3—DOCTORS

GROUP 4—TEACHERS

Figure 5.1
The "fate" map
of your class.

In a similar vein, a cell's "fate" is determined by its position. As you saw in Learning Experience 4, during gastrulation cells move to form three layers. The "fate" of a cell is determined by its position in these layers. For example, cells in the middle or mesoderm layer are destined to become part of muscles, bone, or blood systems of the organism (see Figure 5.2). Because this "fated" cell then divides, its descendants have a similar destiny.

How does this happen? How is the fate of a cell in a specific part of the embryo determined? How does a cell become not only a cell in the circulatory system but a specific kind of cell, a cell of the heart muscle or a red blood cell? Position in the embryo and communication among cells together are the keys in tissue and organ formation. Cells must communicate with their neighbors in order to differentiate into the right kind of cell in the right location.

► ANALYSIS

Write responses to the following in your notebook.

1. Examine the second and third pictures in each of the sequences of embryogenesis on the overhead transparency "Development of Different Organisms." Describe what is happening structurally to the embryo as it develops between these two stages. Describe what you think is happening to the cells between these two stages.

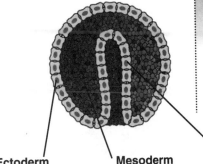

Figure 5.2
The cells at this stage (gastrula) have organized into three layers. Based on their position, cells will develop specialized structures and functions (differentiation).

Ectoderm

- Spinal Cord
- Nerves
- Eye lens
- Hair
- Skin
- Sense organs

Mesoderm

- Bones
- Muscles
- Blood
- Heart
- Kidneys
- Reproductive organs

Endoderm

- Alimentary tract
- Linings of:
    bladder
    respiratory system
    pancreas
    liver
    intestine

2. Imagine that each cell in stage two is a musician in a marching band, a dancer in a ballet troupe, or a member of the medical staff in an operating room. In what ways are these individuals analogous (similar) to cells in a developing embryo?

LOCATION, LOCATION, LOCATION

► ACTIVITY

INTRODUCTION The arrangement of cells in an embryo is of great importance in embryonic development. During gastrulation the cells migrate into positions within the embryo. The fate or future of these cells—that is, what kind of cells they are destined to become—is influenced by their neighboring cells. Thus cells will differentiate into specific kinds of cells based, in part, on their location. You will be forming an Italian flag as a model of the mechanism by which cells may communicate as part of determining how they will specialize.

► MATERIALS NEEDED

For each student:

- 3 sheets of colored paper: one green, one red, one white

► TASK

1. Each of you will "become" a piece of an Italian flag (see Figure 5.3). Take the three sheets of colored paper. Move to an open area of the room and arrange yourself in one of six rows.

Figure 5.3
A model of an Italian
flag with each square
representing a student.

2. Using the illustration above and your location, decide which color paper you should display.

3. Place this color paper on the floor where you are standing and move away. Observe the end result.

READING

POSITION AND DESTINY

How do cells "know" what kind of cell to become in the organism? In making the flag and determining your role, you had to look around you and see where you were relative to everyone else and ask your neighbors about their assessment of the situation. You then chose your colored paper based on that information.

Similarly, cells respond to where they are relative to other cells. Cells acquire information about their position, and then, using this information, express the specific functions needed by a cell in that position. How do cells get this positional information? As you did with your neighbors, cells "talk" or communicate with each other. Cells might do this in several different ways. One way is by chemical communication; a chemical diffuses from one cell to the next. Imagine that the release of this chemical is like someone speaking words. If you are close to the cell that released the chemical, the words might sound like a shout; if you are far away it might sound like a whisper. If a cell is close to the cell sending the chemical message it receives a lot of the chemical; if it is far away it might receive less (or none at all). The amount of this chemical information would help a cell orient itself relative to other cells.

Another type of communication involves direct contact between the membranes of neighboring cells. Small molecules pass between cells in direct contact and this direct contact may be involved in helping cells obtaining positional information. It could be that cells carry out an activity like the game "Telephone" in which a message is whispered from individual to individual. However, in this case, the message might be slightly altered as it is passed along the cellular information highway for determining position.

Once the cell "knows" its position, in a sense, it knows its fate; its position determines what it is destined to become, just as you knew what color you were destined to display in the flag. The cell must then use this information. The DNA within any one cell contains the information that every cell needs to carry out its activities. Once a cell "knows" its position, it expresses the right "color" or segments of DNA (*genes*); the information contained within this DNA enables the cell to develop structures and functions appropriate to its specialized activities. For example, a cell destined to become a red blood cell will make hemoglobin by using the information in the DNA that encodes the information for hemoglobin. This process of development—through which a cell becomes specialized in structure and functions—is called differentiation.

▶ ANALYSIS

Write responses to the following in your notebook.

1. The following events (listed in random order) occur during embryogenesis. Create a flow chart which shows the orderly progression of the early stages of embryogenesis and the processes which occur during this sequence. Since development is a continual process, be sure to show how all the stages and processes interrelate.

    cell communication   differentiation
    blastula   egg
    gastrula   sperm
    cell division   cell location
    undifferentiated cells   fertilized egg
    cell migration   gastrulation
    fertilization

2. How do you think the DNA controls differentiation?

○ In humans, the separation of identical twins may occur after the fertilized egg has undergone several divisions. Yet these twins are identical; every cell contains the same DNA and expresses the same genes. What does this tell you about when the fate of cells is fixed during development? Research what is known about the formation of identical twins.

○ Dr. Victoria Elizabeth Foe is a scientist who has coupled 20th century technology to the time-honored scientific approach of careful observation by connecting an observational microscope to a computer. Using this approach, Dr. Foe can track the journey of a single cell in the blastula to its final destiny in a wing, antenna, or eye of a fruit fly. Her goal is to produce a detailed atlas of embryonic development in a fruit fly, describing the fate of every cell. Research Dr. Foe's work and describe her contributions to our understanding of cell determination and embryonic development. (A very clear and engaging article about Dr. Foe can be found in the chapter "Scientist at Work: Victoria Elizabeth Foe" in *The Beauty of the Beastly*, by Natalie Angier, Houghton Mifflin, 1995.)

○ Embryogenesis produces many organisms that seem, at least at first glance, to be symmetrical; that is, they seem to be a matched set when viewed as two halves divided by a line running down the center of the body. In the case of humans, there are two arms, two legs, two ears, two eyes, and a nose that is more or less the same on either side of this divide. However, in reality, organisms are very asymmetrical. In humans, the heart and spleen are on the left of the body, the liver and gallbladder on the right. The right lung has three lobes, the left only two. How this asymmetry develops is of great interest to embryologists. Current research suggests that asymmetry is the result of polarity created by cells communicating with one another by chemical signaling. Find out about ongoing research and describe how these experiments might explain asymmetry. The article "The Left-Hearted Gene" by Steven Dickman (*Discover Magazine*, August 1996, p. 70) provides an overview of some of this research.

ON THE JOB

EMBRYOLOGIST   Does the idea that every multicellular organism—plant, animal, or insect—develops from one single cell fascinate you? Embryologists are scientists who study the formation, development, structure, and functional activities of an organism in its early stages of development. In addition to observing the growth and division of cells, embryologists look at the sequence of development, investigating how chemical and physical factors influence the growth and development of the organism. The laboratory techniques and procedures used by embryologists are the techniques and tools used by cell biologists, chemists, geneticists, molecular biologists, or physiologists. With a four year college degree, positions as laboratory assistants or research cell biologists are possible. With a master's or doctoral degree, embryologists can teach in a university or pursue independent research in a university or laboratory. Classes such as biology, chemistry, math, English, and computer science are necessary.

TURN ON, TUNE IN, TURN INTO

PROLOGUE   **A**s are all multicellular organisms, you are made up of an impressive collection of different kinds of cells. In humans this includes nerve, blood, skin, muscle, and bone cells (to name a few). All of these cells carry out the same basic activities that are required for maintaining life. In addition to these "housekeeping" functions, these cells also carry out specialized activities which enable them to perform specific functions such as carrying oxygen around the body (in the blood) or protecting the organism from the external environment (the skin). This is *cell specialization.*

What is the origin of this vast variety of cells? When and how do these once identical cells start to become different? These questions have been of great interest to developmental biologists for many years and continue to be one an area of intense and exciting research today.

As you have seen, during the early stages of embryogenesis the fertilized egg divides to produce many daughter cells, each of which contains the same information in the DNA as the original fertilized egg. That leads to a puzzling problem: because all of the cells in the embryo are direct descendants of the original fertilized egg, they must, in theory, carry all the information in the DNA. However, as the organism develops, each cell does not express all of this information. Scientific evidence indicates that at some point in the development process, choices are made about which set of instructions is to be followed. For example, in a cell that is to become a muscle cell, one set of instructions is followed; in a cell destined to become a nerve cell, a different set of instructions is followed.

How does this happen? If a cell contains all the information in its DNA required by the entire organism, how might it be possible to express only some of this information? In this learning experience, you will examine propagation in plants and regeneration in planarians, a flatworm, as models for exploring how differentiation occurs.

HOLD THAT MILK

Specialized cells in the lining of the small intestine of mammals produce the enzyme lactase, which breaks down lactose (the sugar in milk). At birth lactase is produced, enabling the offspring to digest its mother's milk. The production of lactase begins to decline as the animal ages; in humans, this begins to occur between the ages of two and seven. By young adulthood, lactase levels are generally about 10% of what they were during infancy. Despite these lowered levels, most adults can digest lactose and enjoy ice cream, cheese, and other dairy products. However, an inability to digest lactose occurs in many adults whose lactase levels may be just too low for that extra slice of cheese pizza. An intolerance for lactose is very common among certain ethnic groups; 50% of the adults of Hispanic descent and 75% of the adults of African, Asian, and Native American heritage suffer from this problem.

Symptoms of lactose intolerance include abdominal cramping, gas, and diarrhea. Normally, lactose is broken down in the small intestine and the resulting sugars, glucose and galactose, are utilized by cells to synthesize other biomolecules required to sustain life. However, if the lactase levels are low, lactose can pass undigested into the colon where intestinal bacteria use it as a resource for their own metabolic processes.

These bacteria metabolize the lactose to fatty acids, hydrogen, carbon dioxide, and methane. A side effect of this bacterial feast is the retention of water and sodium, which in combination with the gases generated, produce the symptoms characteristic of lactose intolerance.

▶ ANALYSIS

Write responses to the following in your notebook.

1. What can you infer about the information in the DNA for producing the enzyme (protein) lactase in a juvenile?

2. What can you infer about the lactase-producing information in the DNA of a lactose intolerant adult?

3. Based on your answers to questions 1 and 2, give the scientific bases for your inferences.

EXTENDING IDEAS

How is the basic structure of a body determined? What ensures that the head, limbs, and organs will all be located in the proper places? Scientists observed that when fruit flies are exposed to intense X-rays, some of the flies' progeny showed structural anomalies including double sets of wings and legs growing where antennae should be. Investigations showed that X-rays caused mutations in a certain set of genes called Hox genes. Hox genes work in the first few days of embryonic growth to lay out the basic form of the body. Hox genes are found in all animals and their DNA contain sequences which are highly conserved. Research Hox genes and explain current thinking about how these genes are involved in regulating development.

■■▌N THE JOB

BOTANIST   Does the great variety of plants amaze you? Botanists are scientists who study all aspects of plants, including development and life processes, heredity and anatomy. Plant science includes studying organisms such as algae, fungi, lichens, mosses, ferns, conifers, and flowering plants. Botanists might study the whole plant, look at individual cells, try to identify how plants convert chemical compounds from one form into another, or conduct research to identify how the genetic information in DNA controls plant development. With an interest in plant development, a botanist might use plant cell biology and observe the growth and division of cells, or do research in plant breeding or grafting which uses the unique ability of plants to grow entire organisms from a single cell from any part of the plant. Botanists might apply their work to agricultural science. Botanists work in a variety of places, such as botanical gardens, forests, range lands, wilderness areas, museums, industry, government laboratories, and universities. Certain positions involving the care and maintenance of plants in greenhouses, public gardens, and wilderness areas require a two year associates' degree or comparable experience working with plants. With a four year college degree, a botanist can find a position as a laboratory technician or technical assistant. With a master's degree, advanced research positions are available, and with a doctoral degree, it is possible to teach or conduct research at a university. Classes such as English, Latin, foreign languages, math, chemistry, physics, biology, and history are recommended.

Organ-ize

PROLOGUE   The cells are in position and poised for action. They are committed to their roles and prepared to carry out specialized functions. But separate cells cannot achieve the life-sustaining functions required by the organism. Like workers of the world, cells must unite.

During this next phase of embryogenesis, cells having similar or related functions organize into *tissues*. These tissues, in turn, associate with other tissues to form *organs*; organs themselves form *organ systems* that are functionally related and carry out activities needed for life. The organization of cells into tissues, organs, and organ systems requires that cells associate with other cells. As this happens, cells move into the appropriate positions to form tissues, and change shape in order to form the organ. As in gastrulation, all of this requires communication among the cells. Through this communication organs form, organ systems make connections, and the shape of the organism is created.

In this learning experience, you will be examining the organization of plant and animal structures and organs, determining when this organizing occurs during embryogenesis, and investigating external factors that can interfere with the normal development of the structure and function of body systems.

GIMME A ROOT, GIMME A SHOOT

INTRODUCTION   What does a tiny dandelion growing in a grassy field have in common with a towering, giant sequoia in a dense forest? At a casual first glance they seem to have little in common, but on closer observation it becomes quite apparent that despite their size differences the structures of these plants are very similar.

Each plant has roots which anchor the plant into the soil so that it does not wash away, blow down, or fall over. The roots also provide the means by which each plant obtains water and minerals from the soil in which it is growing.

The stem or trunk and branches support the leaves, which are positioned so that they can best carry out their photosynthetic functions—absorbing sunlight for energy and carbon dioxide to manufacture food and releasing oxygen as a byproduct of metabolism. The stem has several transportation roles: It transports water and minerals from the roots to the branches and leaves, and carries food manufactured by the leaves to other parts of the plant.

Also, the tiny dandelion and the massive sequoia are both made up of a wide variety of cell types. These cells are arranged into tissues which are themselves arranged into the roots, stems, and leaves—the plant's "organs."

Each of these organs has a specific function. How does the organization of cells help the plant carry out the functions it requires to sustain life? In the following investigation, you will examine cross sections of plant parts using a microscope. As you observe and describe each plant part, think about how the shape and organization of the cells contribute to the functioning of that particular part.

▶ MATERIALS NEEDED

For each pair of students:
- 2 pairs of safety goggles
- 1 eyedropper
- 3–5 glass microscope slides
- 1 tweezer
- 1 single-edged razor blade
- 1 sheet of cardboard (or other thick paper) as cutting surface
- paper towels
- 1 hand lens

For the class:
- 1 or more full-grown plants (such as geranium, begonia, coleus, ivy, jade, etc.)
- compound or dissecting microscope(s)

- 1 small bottle toluidine blue stain, 0.1% in water
- 2 slide holders for each compound microscope
- prepared slides of root, stem, and leaf tissue (optional)
- prepared slides of several different animal tissues and cell types including epithelial, muscle, blood, cartilage, nerve tissue (optional)
- standard biology textbook (optional)

▶ PROCEDURE

1. Use the eyedropper to place one drop of toluidine blue stain in the center of a clean glass slide.

2. Use the razor blade to cut a piece of stem from the plant provided. On the cutting surface, cut a 0.5–1 mm cross-section slice from the stem piece.

3. Use the tweezer to place the cross-section next to the drop of stain making sure that the stain touches only one end of the cross-section. Let the piece stand for 10-30 seconds.

4. Apply a corner of a paper towel to the edge of the drop of stain in order to absorb excess stain. Do not move the cross-section slice on the slide.

5. Place the slide on the stage of the dissecting microscope and observe it. If you are using a compound microscope, invert the slide (section side down) propped on the craft stick slide holders on the stage of the microscope (see Figure 7.1).

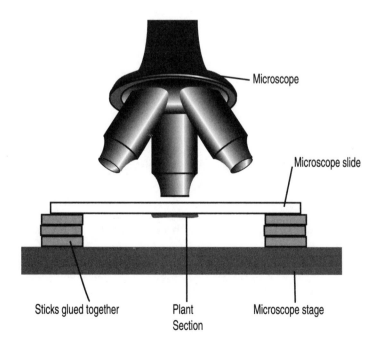

Microscope

Microscope slide

Sticks glued together   Plant Section   Microscope stage

Figure 7.1
Diagram of slide on holder.

6. STOP & THINK Observe the cross-section of the stem under the microscope. Describe/draw the patterns or designs of the cell types you see in your notebook. (See Figure 7.2 for examples of how tissues are organized in plants.)

7. Cut a cross-section of the root from the plant and repeat steps 1–6.

8. Cut a leaf cross-section and repeat steps 1–6. Try cutting leaf sections in different ways.

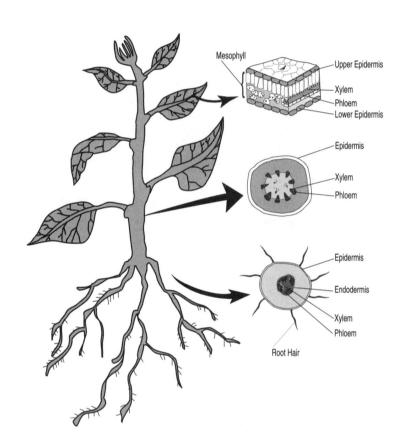

Figure 7.2
Schematic cross-sections of plant parts.

▶ **ANALYSIS**

Write responses to the following in your notebooks.

1. How many different cell types did you observe in the stem? in the leaf? in the root?

2. How do the different patterns you observed in the different parts of the plant compare?

3. Based on the description of plant part functions in the introduction to this activity, describe how you think the shapes and arrangements of the cells you observed might relate to the function of the part.

INTERNAL DEVELOPMENT AND EXTERNAL FACTORS

Embryogenesis is a period of dramatic and rapidly occurring events in the life of an organism. If it were a film being viewed in fast forward, embryonic development would be seen as an astonishing extravaganza of movement, growth, pattern formation, change, and construction involving a cast of millions.

FROM CELLS TO ORGANS

As you have seen, the earliest stages of vertebrate development involve extensive cell division and movement into position with little increase in the size of the organism. Then, the developing organism begins to increase in size and cells begin to differentiate into their specialized functions from specific regions of the gastrula. Cells with similar and related functions next associate into tissues which, in turn, begin to form organs by folding and bending into shapes characteristic of a heart, a brain, or a liver. As this formation occurs the cells themselves take on shapes characteristic of their specialized functions.

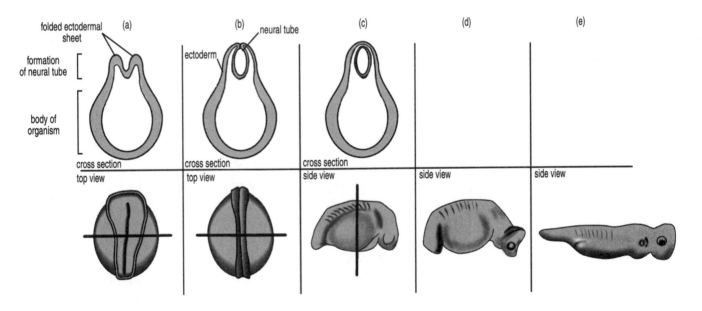

Figure 7.3
Illustration of neural tube formation in amphibians. The top row represents cross-sections of the organism made at the line drawn through the illustration of the whole organism (bottom row). Formation of the brain and spinal cord develops when the upper surface of the embryo flattens into a broad plate bounded by two folds (a). These folds rise up and meet each other and fuse, forming the neural tube that will be the spinal cord (b). The folds fuse and the tube settles below the surface and is covered by a sheet of cells that will form the skin (c). The brain continues to develop as does the rest of the organism (d, e).

Organ and organ system formation involves cell movement, cell association into sheets, and folding. Communication among cells is essential in all of these processes; the interactions and recognition events that occur among cells ensure that cells will be in the right place, at the right time. Much of organ formation involves the folding of cell sheets. The folding is the result primarily of a series of coordinated and carefully timed changes in the shape of cells which cause the sheet to bend and fold. Folding of cell sheets forms the basis of development for many organs including the heart, lungs, brain, eyes, and teeth (see Figure 7.3 on the previous page).

HUMAN GESTATION

Figure 7.4 illustrates the major developmental events of human gestation, which lasts about nine months. During the first eight weeks the embryo has increased in mass about 500 times and is about an inch long. The embryo has organized into its characteristic human shape and the organs are formed and in place. From this time on, the embryo in humans is referred to as a *fetus*. Fetal development (from 9 weeks to 40 weeks) primarily involves growth and maturation; the fetus increases in size, its body shape becomes more defined, and the organ systems mature in structure and function.

Although human embryogenesis is usually very successful, during certain time periods the process is acutely sensitive to external factors that can interfere with the sequence of events. The chart of human embryogenesis (Figure 7.4) indicates periods in which the embryo and fetus are susceptible to external factors that may cause morphological (structural) and functional defects.

The period of greatest susceptibility is very early in embryogenesis (the first few weeks) when the cells are dividing rapidly and laying the foundations for organ and system development, skeletal structure, and body shape. If damage or change occurs during this period, a time when many women are unaware that they are pregnant, the consequences are magnified and can be devastating—often fatal. Damage during this critical early period affects the morphology of limbs and organs, and these defects in the morphology generally impair the proper functioning of these systems.

A simple analogy for the extensive damage that can occur during early embryogenesis can be seen in the game "Telephone." In this game one person whispers a message to another person. A second person whispers this message to another individual who then transmits the message to yet another person and so on. If an error in communication occurs early in the game, many individuals will have the incorrect information, whereas if an error occurs late in the game, only a few individuals are affected.

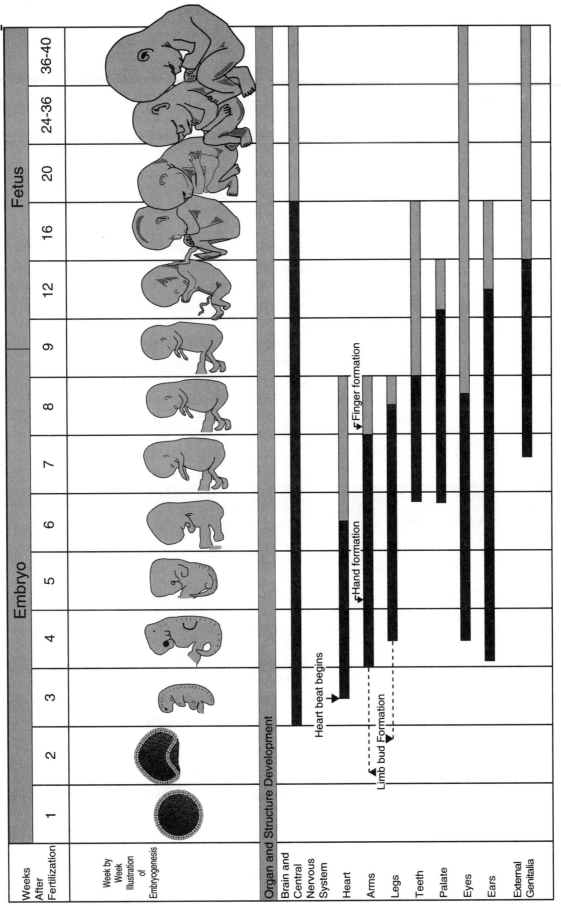

Figure 7.4 *HUMAN EMBRYOGENESIS*

Indicates period susceptible to major morphological defects.

Indicates period susceptible to functional defects.

Later in development, when organ systems are maturing, functional and minor morphological defects can occur. Errors that occur during these later stages of embryogenesis, while serious, generally have less extensive consequences. (Errors in the newly born human are referred to as *birth defects*.)

While some birth defects are the result of inherited errors in genetic information, many defects can be caused by factors in the environment such as pollutants, drugs, chemicals, alcohol, and infectious agents; these agents are termed *teratogens* (literally, monster-making). When a pregnant woman is exposed to these teratogens in her food, medicine, or drugs, in the air she breathes, or by direct skin contact, these compounds may make their way to the embryo or fetus and affect the pattern of development. Even the egg and sperm of the parents can be damaged by certain chemicals prior to fertilization. Some researchers suggest that the large amounts of synthetic chemicals in the environment have contributed to a significant decrease in the production of human sperm in recent years (one study indicates a fall of 50% between 1940 and 1990) and the increasing occurrence of infertility. Table 7.5 lists some of the external factors that can affect embryogenesis in humans.

Table 7.5
External factors that affect human embryological development.

EXTERNAL FACTOR	SITE OF ACTION	PERIOD OF SUSCEPTIBILITY IN GESTATION	POTENTIAL PROBLEM OR OUTCOME IN INFANT
thalidomide	prevents vascularization of the embryo	3–6 weeks	arms and legs do not develop; malformed organs of digestive and circulatory systems
rubella virus (German measles)	crosses placenta; infects fetus	12–16 weeks	deafness; mental impairment
methyl mercury	brain	late gestation	brain dysfunction
drugs	direct action on central nervous system and brain of the fetus	throughout gestation period (9 months)	seizures; irritability; addiction
cigarettes	reduced oxygen consumption by mother; mild depressant of central nervous system of the fetus	throughout gestation period (9 months)	growth deficiency; low birth weight
alcohol	brain	throughout gestation period (9 months)	growth deficiency; mental impairment; structural abnormalities
malnutrition	availability of nutrients to the fetus	mid to late gestation	low birth weight

▶ ANALYSIS

Write responses to the following in your notebook in preparation for a class discussion. Use Figure 7.4 and Table 7.5 to aid you in your responses.

1. In Learning Experience 1—Those Terrible Blue Tablets, you read about the devastating effects of thalidomide on the development of infants. Use your knowledge of embryogenesis to explain how the action of thalidomide may have caused the defects.

2. How do you think each external factor causes the defect described in Table 7.5 and why does it have its effects during certain periods of embryogenesis?

3. Using "external factors" as the key concept, construct a concept map that shows the effect of at least three external factors on the embryo/fetus. What conclusions can you draw about the susceptibility of an embryo to external factors?

4. Imagine that you are a medical practitioner and a woman has come to you early in her pregnancy for advice on what she can do to have a healthy baby. Describe what you would say to her regarding her diet, life style, what things to do and what things to avoid. Include a clear explanation of development that would justify your advice.

Any Drink During Pregnancy May Be One Too Many

LATEST RESEARCH INTO FETAL ALCOHOL SYNDROME SHOWS

by Jane E. Brody, New York Times *News Service, February 23, 1986.*

In the Old Testament, Samson's mother is admonished by an angel: "Thou shalt conceive, and bear a son. Now therefore beware, I pray thee, and drink not wine nor strong drink."

In ancient Carthage, the law forbade bridal couples to drink on their wedding night. And in 1834, a report to the British House of Commons noted that infants born to alcoholic mothers had "a starved, shriveled and imperfect look." But it was not until 1973 that medical scientists confirmed what people seem to have known for thousands of years: that alcohol consumed by a pregnant woman can damage her unborn child. That year two pediatric researchers from the University of Washington in Seattle rediscovered and named fetal alcohol syndrome.

At first it was thought that only the offspring of heavy-drinking alcoholic mothers were at risk. Now it is known that even as little as two drinks a week may do damage, and knowledgeable physicians recommend that women abstain completely from alcohol from the moment they start trying to conceive until they are finished nursing.

Even women who drank during previous pregnancies with no apparent ill effect on their offspring are cautioned against assuming that subsequent children will be similarly spared.

So widespread and serious are the potential consequences of alcohol on the unborn child that Congress has designated this week National Fetal Alcohol Syndrome Awareness Week. The goal is to make every woman of childbearing age aware of the danger and persuade her to refrain from alcohol for the sake of her unborn child. Despite educational efforts since the mid-'70s, it is estimated that 50,000 babies were born last year with permanent harm from prenatal alcohol exposure.

THE DAMAGE DONE

Fetal alcohol syndrome, or FAS, is a cluster of severe physical and mental defects caused by alcohol damage to the developing fetus. While the defects vary from baby to baby, these are the most common major abnormalities:

- Growth retardation before and after birth, with no catching up later even if the baby is well-nourished. FAS children are typically small and thin.
- Facial malformations, including small, widely spaced eyes; short, upturned nose with a wide, flat bridge; flat cheeks; narrow upper lip that lacks a vertical groove, and a blunt, small chin that may appear large and pointed as the child gets older.
- Brain damage, including an abnormally small head and brain; mild to moderate mental retardation (I.Q. is usually 60 to 75); hyperactivity; poor coordination, and learning disabilities.
- Abnormal development of various body organs, including heart defects; underdeveloped genitals in girls; urinary tract and kidney defects, among others.

The full-blown syndrome is most likely to afflict the children of alcoholic mothers who drink heavily, especially early in pregnancy when the fetal organs are forming. From 40 to 50 percent of the babies of heavy drinkers are born with FAS.

Most of the other affected babies, including many born to far more moderate consumers of alcohol, may suffer more subtle fetal alcohol effects. These include small size (again with no catching up after birth), reduced intelligence, learning disabilities, hyperactivity, eye and speech problems and sometimes organ abnormalities. During the newborn period these babies tend to be restless, have sleep problems, cry often and uncontrollably and otherwise act in ways that could impair the mother-infant bond.

A study at Emory University in Atlanta showed behavioral problems in babies born to women who drank as few as two drinks a week throughout pregnancy. The babies appeared more agitated and stressed, less in control of their bodies and less responsive to people and the environment. The behavioral defects persisted at least to one year of age and appear to be permanent. In addition, several studies have shown that mothers who drink during pregnancy, even as little as two drinks a week, are more likely to have miscarriages and stillbirths.

FACTS TO REMEMBER

Several sources, including the American Medical Association in an excellent pamphlet, "Alcohol & Pregnancy: Why They Don't Mix," have made these observations and warnings:

A pregnant woman is literally drinking for two. Alcohol readily crosses the placenta and reaches the same concentration in the fetal blood and body cells as in the mother's.

Some of the most devastating consequences of alcohol occur during the early weeks of pregnancy, before many women even know they are pregnant. Experts recommend that women stop drinking when pregnancy is possible, rather than waiting until conception is confirmed.

Alcohol is nothing but empty calories. Even if it did not cause malformation of the fetus, it would be unwise for a pregnant woman to drink. She is better off consuming a nutritious liquid such as fruit juice or milk.

There is no known safe level of alcohol intake during pregnancy. While alcohol's effects are clearly dose-related (higher intakes are associated with more severe damage), even a small amount of alcohol consumed at the wrong time may affect fetal development adversely.

Fetal damage caused by alcohol cannot be detected prenatally through amniocentesis, so there is no way to find out before birth whether the fetus has been harmed.

No form of alcohol is safer than another. Neither beer nor wine is less damaging than hard liquor.

Even drinking before pregnancy may have an untoward result. Research at the University of Washington showed that mothers who had about one drink a day before pregnancy tended to have smaller babies.

Fathers' drinking, too, may have untoward effects. Men who drink heavily are not only more likely to be impotent but also have lower sperm counts and lower sex-hormone levels. One animal study showed that when males were given alcohol before mating with alcohol-free females, there were fewer live births and the offspring were smaller.

The fetal damage wrought by alcohol occurs independently of the effects of smoking, poor nutrition, poverty, illness and exposure to other drugs. So alcohol effects can occur even if the mother is a well-nourished, healthy nonsmoker.

Fetal alcohol damage seems to be permanent. No amount of good nutrition and postnatal care erase the growth retardation and brain damage.

The effects of alcohol on a fetus are highly variable. Other factors, including genetics, clearly play a role. For example, in a case involving non-identical twins, one was born with fetal alcohol syndrome and the other was much less severely affected.

Continued on next page

Many cases of prenatal alcohol damage go undetected. Experts estimate that for every child with FAS, at least 10 others have more subtle and often unrecognized alcohol-caused problems. Indeed, prenatal alcohol exposure may turn out to be a primary cause of learning disabilities and hyperactivity.

Some of the distressing behavioral results in newborns can be averted if a woman stops drinking by the sixth month of pregnancy. Even a single drink toward the end of pregnancy can temporarily stop "breathing" movements by the unborn child [fetus].

Alcohol also may hurt infant development when exposure occurs after birth. A nursing mother who drinks can pass the alcohol to the baby through her milk. Thus it is wisest to wait until weaning before resuming alcohol consumption.

EXTENDING IDEAS

- Spina bifida is a relatively common birth defect (occurring in about one in a thousand live births) in which the neural tube fails to fuse during development and part of the spinal cord is left exposed. If left untreated, the affected infant may die or be left with severe disabilities. Pregnant women who supplement their diets with a B vitamin, folic acid, can reduce their risk of having a baby with spina bifida. Although how folic acid works is still not completely understood, recent research suggests it may involve methylation of an amino acid. Find out about this research and what the data suggests.

- Accutane (a brand name for the chemical isotretinoin) is a drug widely used to control acne. It is known that Accutane can cause birth defects and yet the Food and Drug Administration has decided to permit it to remain on the market. Research the FDA's decision on this and determine what evidence was used to determine its safety and hazards and why the decision was made to keep Accutane on the market.

- *The Broken Cord* by Michael Dorris (New York: Harper & Row, 1989) tells of his adoption of a Native American boy and his search to discover the cause of his son's sometimes uncontrollable behavior and mental limitations. This well-written and riveting book was one of the first to call attention to the tragedy of fetal alcohol syndrome. Read *The Broken Cord* and relate Adam's symptoms and behaviors to your knowledge of the susceptibility of the human embryo to the external factor of alcohol.

- Cell death, a normal part of development, is involved in molding the overall body shape. It helps to sculpt the form of the limb; in mice and humans the digits are joined together in a paddle-like structure early in development and the death of some of these cells allows the individual digits to form. The tail, present early in mammal embryogenesis and in the tadpole, disappears as a result of cell death. This kind of cell death, called apoptosis, is not due to aging or sickness but rather is a programmed event in the development sequence. Research what is known about apoptosis and the role it plays in development and in other life processes.

ON THE JOB

DRUG/ALCOHOL ADDICTION COUNSELOR   Does the idea of helping someone with a drug or alcohol problem appeal to you? Drug/Alcohol addiction counselors help those with addiction problems get access to treatment. Counselors need to be able to deal with crisis situations, be skilled at interviewing, know how to use available treatment resources and develop new ones, and be able to participate in formulating treatment plans. Drug/Alcohol addiction counselors might work on an inpatient unit, in a day or evening treatment program, or be part of an outpatient clinic. A minimum of an associates' degree along with special certification as an addiction treatment counselor is required. For those with more advanced degrees, there are additional counselor positions available. Beginning in high school such classes as sociology, public health, psychology, biology and communication are helpful.

HISTOLOGY TECHNICIAN   Would you be interested in using your organizational and detail-oriented skills working in the medical field? Histology technicians prepare thin sections of body tissues which physicians, surgeons or pathologists use to diagnose and treat disease. Technicians freeze and cut sections of tissue, mount the section onto slides and then stain the cells to make certain details more visible. Histology technicians might work in a hospital, for-profit laboratory, a clinic, or a public health care facility. Not all positions are in health care; some opportunities are in veterinary pathology, marine biology, forensic pathology or in industrial research. Histology technicians might have either a high school diploma with one or two years of post high school education in a histologic technology certification program or a two year college degree in histologic technology. With a four year college degree and one year of experience, advancement to a histotechnologist is possible. This means performing more complex techniques, teaching, being a laboratory supervisor or directing a school for histologic technology. All laboratory technicians are certified. Classes such as biology, chemistry, math, computer science, and English are useful.

Ready [or Not], Here I Come!

PROLOGUE **W**hen does embryogenesis end? Do all organisms emerge into the world only when they are ready to be independent, or do some emerge earlier? What determines when the prenatal state is over? In this learning experience, you will explore the various states of development in which different organisms enter the world and what it means to be "independent" in the biological sense.

Are Babies Born as Embryos?

READING

In his essay "Human Babies as Embryos," Stephen Jay Gould describes two basic reproductive strategies of mammals.

Some mammals. . . have brief gestations [short pregnancies] and give birth to large litters of poorly developed young (tiny, hairless, helpless, and with unopened eyes and ears). . . [These mammals (called altricial) tend to have short life spans and brains that are small relative to their body size. . . The other kind has] long gestations, long life spans, big brains,. . . and give birth to a few, well-developed babies capable, at least in part, of fending for themselves at birth. . . [Primates are typical of this latter group (called precocial).]. . . Relative to body sizes, brains are the biggest and gestation times and life spans are longest among mammals. Litter size, in most cases, has been reduced to the absolute minimum of one. Babies are well developed and capable at birth. However. . . we encounter one obviously glaring and embarrassing exception—namely us. We share most of the precocial characteristics with our primate cousins—long life, large brains, and small litters. But our babies are as helpless and undeveloped at birth as those of most altricial mammals. . . Why did this most precocial of all species in some traits (notably the brain) evolve a baby far less developed and more helpless than that of its primate ancestors?

I will propose an answer to this question that is bound to strike most readers as patently absurd: Human babies are born as embryos, and embryos they remain for about the first nine months of life. If women gave birth when they "should"—after a gestation of about a year and a half—our babies would share the standard precocial features of other primates. . .

Gould goes on to describe the general patterns of embryonic development and growth that remain incomplete before human birth. He describes a certain stage of bone growth that is completed several weeks before birth in some monkeys, but in humans is completed only years after birth. But perhaps most important is the extent to which the human brain grows after birth. The brains of many mammals are essentially fully formed at birth, but the brain of a newborn human is only one-fourth its adult size.

. . . But why are human babies born before their time? Why has evolution extended our general development so greatly, but held our gestation time in check, thereby giving us an essentially embryonic baby? Why was gestation not equally prolonged with the rest of development?

Gould goes on to answer his own question:

. . . I do not think it can be denied that human birth is difficult compared with that of most other mammals. To put it rather grossly, it's a tight squeeze. We know that female primates can die in attempted childbirth when fetal heads are too large to pass through the pelvic canal. . . There are not, I am confident, many human females who could give birth successfully to a year-old baby.

The culprit in this tale is our most important evolutionary specialization, our large brain. In most mammals, brain growth is entirely a fetal phenomenon. But since the brain never gets very large, this poses no problem for birth. . . Human brains, however, are so large that another strategy must be added for a successful birth—gestation must be shortened relative to general development, and birth must occur when the brain is only one-fourth its final size . . .

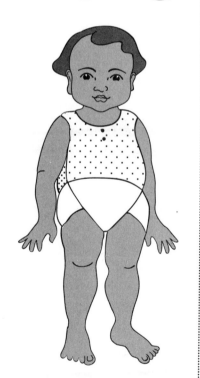

Figure 8.1
Comparison of newborn and one-year-old child.

► ANALYSIS

Write responses to the following in your notebook.

1. Using your understandings about biology, explain the reasoning that Gould uses to justify his belief that human babies are born as embryos.

2. What do you think are the social and biological implications of babies being born developmentally early? Identify as many factors as possible.

Born Too Soon?

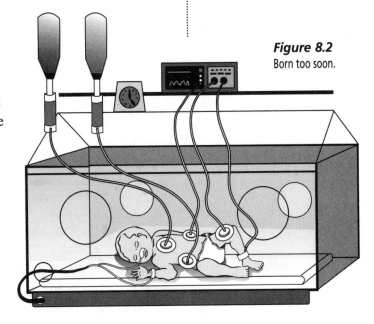

► READING

The lights are dim and soothing and the room quiet despite the constant hum of equipment in the background night and day. With apprehensive excitement, the new parents approach the small, plastic box which holds their baby who, for some reason, was born 10 weeks too soon. The fears for their newborn's health mix with their desires to hold and comfort her. Peering in, at first all they see is machinery—tubes coming from her nose to machines which provide her with life-sustaining nutrients, tubes coming from her arms, wires monitoring her heartbeat and breathing, the incubator which provides the warmth and oxygen her body requires and cannot obtain for itself. Then they see the baby beneath the tubing and again are startled; this is not the chubby baby of the diaper and baby food commercials, or of the baby books they have been reading. This baby is wizened and looks old, not baby-like at all.

Figure 8.2
Born too soon.

In fact, she looks more like pictures of a developing fetus. But, moving closer to the incubator, the parents look again. Focusing on the child, their child, they discover that she does have their features: her father's complexion, her mother's profile. She is definitely their baby, after all.

No one knows exactly why some babies are born earlier than they should be. In some cases, a pregnant woman's consumption of too much alcohol or too little nutritious food may cause her baby to be born before the full 40 weeks of growth in the womb (gestation) that is normal. But most times there is no explanation. Too little time in the womb means too little time spent growing in this most favorable environment.

The final months of gestation are critical in human development. Although the major morphological features (form and structures) have formed, and many organ systems have developed and begun to function prior to this time, significant development still needs to occur. This period is a time of substantial weight gain, essential in developing the strength and fat reserves that the newborn will require. In addition to growth, vital developmental events occur during these later stages: lungs develop the ability to take up oxygen; and the brain continues to develop, even well beyond birth. Significant changes in the morphology of the brain occur during the last two months. Figure 8.3 illustrates the massive increase in convolutions or wrinkling that occurs in the cortex of the brain between the seventh and ninth months; this wrinkling is the result of extensive cell division during which millions of new nerve cells are added to the developing human brain each minute. This growth greatly increases the surface area of the brain; it is this area of the brain in which thinking and recognition occurs and imparts those qualities and characteristics that we think of as human.

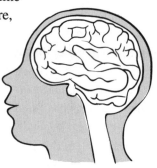

The earlier a baby is born "before its time" the less developed these essential systems are, and the more support the baby will need to survive outside the womb. Modern technology has made it possible for even very premature babies to survive. The incubator acts as a kind of "halfway house" for a baby making the transition from the total physical dependence of the womb to the independence of being a separate individual. Machines and tubes will help it breathe, obtain nutrients, and respond to its needs and environment until its own organ systems are developed enough to take over.

Figure 8.3
Changes in the wrinkling of the brain between the seventh and ninth months of gestation.

THE ENDPOINT

The baby just described was born too soon. How do organisms "know" when the time has come? At some point in the life of every organism, development within the protected environment of the womb, or egg, or seed ends. For many organisms this endpoint—which culminates in birth, or hatching, or germination—marks the time when the essential systems have developed sufficiently to sustain life functions in the environment where the organism will live. The organism at this point is capable of obtaining and utilizing resources from this environment and is able to respond to both internal needs and external influences.

Little is understood about what signals developing organisms that their time has come to face the world. It may be that a combination of exhaustion of the food supply of the egg, womb, or seed and the developmental readiness for independence serve to signal the organism that its "birthday" has arrived. But who decides to break that ultimate of bonds—the mother or the child? Recent research on sheep suggests that the fetal brain keeps track of its own development, and when the fetus is ready for birth, it sends chemical signals (hormones) to the mother. The mother's own system then prepares for birth. Scientists hope that this kind of understanding may help in developing methods to prevent premature birth and parental anguish.

Organisms display a wide range of "readiness" when they leave the safety of the egg, the womb, or the seed. Many mammals are born "ready to roll." The newborn elephant, the horse, and the fallow deer are up on their feet within minutes, feeding within the hour, and running with the pack in days. Yet other mammals are born in a very helpless, embryonic state (see Figure 8.4). Mouse babies are hairless and helpless for several days after birth. A kangaroo joey leaves the birth canal little more than a centimeter long; it is blind and naked; the hind legs and tail are mere buds. However, its front legs have developed large clawed hands, and by using these hands, it climbs into its mother's pouch, where it finds shelter and nutrients to help it complete its embryogenesis in an external, yet safe, environment. Birds show a wide range of developmental readiness at hatching. A hen's chick can run and feed itself soon after hatching, but a newly hatched sparrow or robin is naked, has its eyes closed, and is helpless. It can open its beak and receive nutrients that it may have left the egg to find, but can do little else until further development occurs.

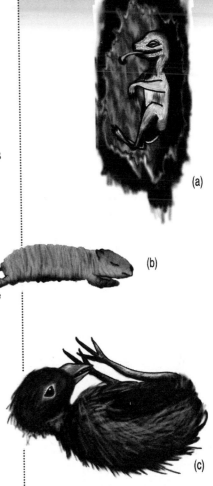

(a)

(b)

(c)

Figure 8.4
Examples of newborn animals: a kangaroo joey (a), a mouse (b), and a bird (c).

VARIATIONS ON A THEME

The appearance of many organisms changes dramatically from the moment when they enter the world to when they are adults. One of the most studied examples is the frog. The frog emerges from the egg in the form of a tadpole that immediately begins to feed and swim. Yet this form continues to develop significantly after hatching: great changes occur in its shape and structures as the organism continues to mature to adulthood.

The creature emerging from an insect egg may have one of three forms. Primitive

Figure 8.5
Are the two animals at the left related?

insects, such as silverfish, hatch out as miniature adults: they grow to adulthood simply by molting or splitting their old skins when they become too tight. Thus from the time it leaves the egg until death, the insect is fairly much the same, except for the fact that it slowly grows larger as it gets older.

A second kind of pattern displayed by insects upon hatching is the emergence of a nymph, an organism that resembles the adult in most respects, but lacks certain adult features, such as wings or the ability to breathe air. These are structures that develop as part of the maturation toward adulthood. The harlequin cabbage bug, a stink bug, changes from nymph to adult mainly by the acquisition of wings.

The third pattern in insects is that of complete change, or *metamorphosis*. In this case, the larva that emerges from the egg is distinctly different from the adult, often living in a different environment and having different habits. The painted lady butterfly begins life as a crawling caterpillar feeding on leaves. It then enters a chrysalis, or cocoon, stage before emerging as a delicate and very different creature, the butterfly, which feeds on the nectar of flowers.

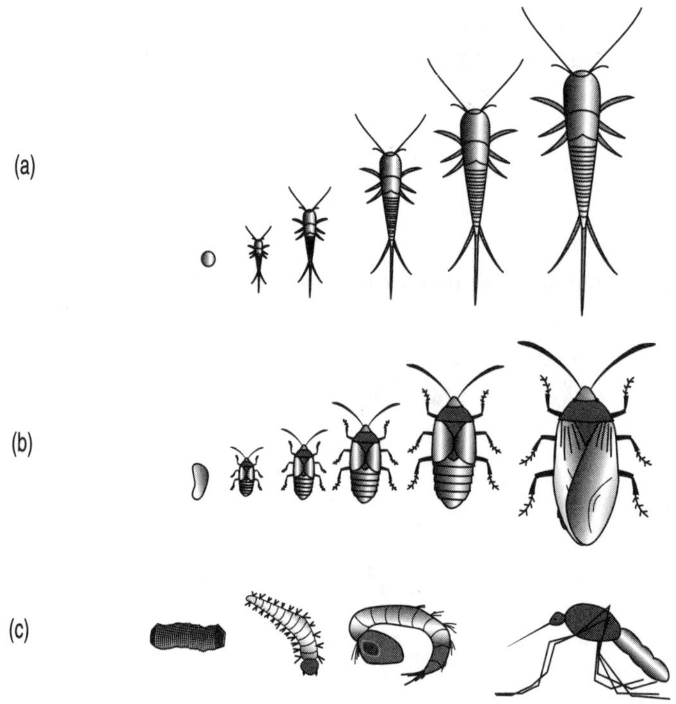

Figure 8.6
Patterns of change in insects from egg to adult: (a) no change—insects emerge as miniature adults (silverfish); (b) incomplete metamorphosis—insects emerge resembling adults, and develop new structures as they mature (beetle); (c) metamorphosis—insect form emerging from egg is completely different from the adult stage (mosquito).

(a)

(b)

(c)

Seed *germination* is a form of plant "birth." In patterns similar to animal development, a fertilized egg is formed by the union of pollen and egg within the ovary of the flower. Within the seed coat, the embryonic plant develops the specialized cells, structures and systems that it will require to live independently in the world. When the time is right, the ovary (or fruit) ripens and splits, releasing its seed. Unlike animals, which give birth or hatch within a short time period, seeds can remain dormant for long periods of time; that is, germination does not necessarily happen when a seed leaves the ovary of the plant. When the level of moisture in the environment is right, when abrasion of the seed occurs in its passing through the intestinal system of an animal, or when the presence of oxygen is sensed, germination may occur. The ability of plants to detect the appropriateness of their environment for growth is essential, because once plants have set down roots, they have no easy way of moving if the environment is not right. Plants germinate as seedlings, small plants with roots and embryonic leaves. These seedlings quickly develop true leaves and soon resemble small adults which will continue to grow.

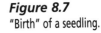

Figure 8.7
"Birth" of a seedling.

All organisms grow and show changes after birth. In some, such as mammals and plants, the changes are greater between fertilization and birth than between birth and maturity. In other organisms, such as frogs and insects, tremendous change occurs after they emerge from the egg and progress to adulthood. From a development and growth perspective it is not clear why this range of variation occurs. The explanation may lie in the environment in which these organisms live or in how these organisms evolved.

▶ ANALYSIS

Write responses to the following in your notebook.

1. Describe the differences and similarities among being "born too soon" as described in the beginning of the essay, being born in an immature state as in the case of the kangaroo joey, and being born as a human embryo, as Stephen Jay Gould describes.

2. Compare a silverfish, a frog, a joey, and a human baby. What characteristics would all these organisms share when they were fully independent?

3. Create a new flow chart of embryogenesis. This exercise is designed to enable you to order the ideas and concepts presented so far in this module into a cohesive, sequential explanation of the process of embryonic development. Use all of the concepts listed in the margin in your chart.

CONCEPTS FOR FLOW CHART
cell communication
blastula
sperm
cell location
cell migration
fertilization
cell commitment
common descent
species DNA
organs
hatching
maturation
differentiation
egg
gastrula
undifferentiated cells
specialized cells
fertilized egg
selected expression of DNA
ancestral DNA
organ systems
tissues
birth
cell division
germination
gastrulation

EXTENDING IDEAS

○ Scientists have succeeded in isolating immature eggs from the ovaries of a newborn mouse; these eggs were then allowed to develop to maturity and then fertilized *in vitro* (in a test tube). Once the eggs reached the two-cell embryo stage, they were inserted into a female mouse and allowed to develop. Of 190 embryo implantations, only two mice gave birth (from "First Mammal Born from Lab-Grown Egg Cell," *Science News*, January 27, 1996, p. 54). The implications of this research are many; it would permit the study of immature egg development, the testing of compounds that may cause birth defects and the development of new contraceptives. On a more hypothetical level it would provide breeders and conservation biologists a valuable and rapid new way to generate offspring from farm animals and endangered species. One of the researchers described it as a way to produce large numbers of animals from a fetus before that fetus would ever be old enough to give birth. Describe how this technology could achieve all of the intended uses.

○ When are you old enough to leave home? According to a recent study perhaps you never really do, at least not completely. Investigators have found that during pregnancy fetal cells may escape into the bloodstream of the mother, and descendants of these cells may persist for many years after the birth of the child. An article in *Science News* ("Kids: Getting Under Mom's Skin for Decades", February 10, 1996, p. 85) describes this research and the implications. Describe the experimental design of this experiment and indicate how the data supported these conclusions. Then figure out a way to explain to your mother (or anyone's mother) about the maternal tie that binds. . . and binds. . . and binds.

ON THE JOB

MIDWIFE   Would you like to help bring babies into the world who are healthy and wanted? Midwives attend over 70% of the births that take place in the world and are in growing demand in the United States. The role of the midwife begins long before the moment of birth and continues after the child is delivered. Midwives provide prenatal care by monitoring the health of the mother and the progress of the fetus, providing mothers-to-be with important advice about nutrition and exercise, and supporting the parents as they prepare for delivery. After the delivery, the midwife may provide postpartum support, education, and health care for the mother and baby during the first few weeks. Many midwives provide family planning services and routine women's health care such as pap smears, physical exams, information on sexually transmitted diseases, and assistance and support during menopause. Some midwives provide health counseling and education for entire families. The range of services that a midwife can provide in the United States is dependent on the educational experiences he or she has had and the state of residence. There are different paths to becoming a midwife. Some training programs require a degree in nursing and others will accept a liberal arts degree with coursework in biology and health sciences.

NEONATAL OR MATERNITY NURSE   Do you think you might be interested in caring for newborn babies who were born too soon? Neonatal nurses are health care professionals who work in hospitals to provide special treatment for critically ill premature infants. Maternity nurses help in the delivery room, take care of newborns and teach mothers how to feed and care for their babies. Like all nurses, these specialists work in collaboration with physicians and other members of a health care team to assess and monitor the condition of a patient and then to develop and implement a plan of health care. Nurses might work in a hospital or in another health care facility such as a physician's office, at a public health agency, school, camp or for a Health Maintenance Organization (HMO). With additional training to expand skills and knowledge, registered nurses may become nurse practitioners and do many tasks previously handled by physicians (such as making diagnoses and recommending medications). With a master's degree registered nurses may become clinical nursing specialists and focus in one field of nursing (for example, working in the neonatal unit). There are several different program sequences that provide nursing training. With a two year program in nursing, it is possible to work in any of the settings described above. With a four year college degree in nursing it is possible to hold an administrative position or work for a public health agency. With a master's degree it is possible to specialize or to teach in a school of nursing. In all cases, nurses must pass a licensing exam before they are registered nurses and can practice nursing. Classes in subjects such as biology, chemistry, math, physics, and English are useful.

GROWING, GROWING...

PROLOGUE   **W**hat happens after an organism emerges into the world? In the last learning experience, you saw that organisms vary in their readiness to be independent in the world; some emerge ready to fly or run while others, such as humans, require continued development of their immune and nervous systems after birth. However after birth or hatching or germination, almost all life forms continue to develop and grow.

In this learning experience, you will explore the changes in organisms after birth or germination. You will examine the developmental events which occur between birth and adulthood in humans and you will explore growth as a pivotal and carefully controlled process of these stages of life, using plant growth as a model system.

WILL MY INVESTMENT GROW?

INTRODUCTION   What controls patterns of growth of an organism? What factors might determine how an organism grows? In this learning experience, you will have the opportunity to explore how growth patterns can be controlled and even altered.

Imagine the following scenario: A small biotechnology company has developed a compound and claims that it affects how plants grow. If the compound is applied near the growing tip (*apical stem*) of the plant, the plant grows taller than it would without the compound. The company has convinced investors that the taller the plant, the greater the profits to be made from that plant. You must decide whether or not you should invest in this company.

You will be provided with a compound which has been isolated from plants. Your group's task is to design and carry out an experiment to test the compound on pea plants. Plan your procedure with your group members using only the materials available.

▶ MATERIALS NEEDED

For each group of four students:
- 4 pairs of safety goggles
- 2 two-week-old seedlings of variety A pea plant
- 2 two-week-old seedlings of variety B pea plant
- 4 toothpicks
- metric measuring tape
- graph paper or graphing software (such as Cricketgraph)

For the class:
- lanolin paste with the "secret" compound
- lanolin paste alone

▶ PROCEDURE

1. As you and your group think about the design of your experiment be sure that you agree on:
   - the question that is being asked
   - a hypothesis
   - the procedure to be used to carry out the experiment (list the steps)
   - the control (positive or negative)
   - the method to be used for recording growth
   - the type of data that will be collected
   - how you will collect your data and how often
   - how you will record your data
   - what kind of analysis you will make of your data
   - any safety precautions to be taken

2. When your group has designed the experiment, have your teacher check it before beginning the experiment. Be prepared to explain your reasoning and, if necessary, to make adjustments or changes.

3. Carry out the experiment according to your group's design, while keeping records and gathering data in each of your notebooks.

4. At the conclusion of the experiment, conduct a final analysis of the experiment and write a laboratory report using your group's protocol, data, and the information requested in Learning Experience 11, "Did My Investment Grow?"

Apical stem

Figure 9.1
New growth in a plant occurs at the apical stem or growing tip of the plant. To test any compound for effects on growth, it is best to apply it to this tip.

Growing Up Is Hard to Do

The period between birth and adulthood is a time of change and growth. Certain organisms, such as frogs and butterflies, change dramatically in appearance to the point where the juvenile stage bears little resemblance to the adult stage; in other organisms, such as mammals, the juvenile and adult are similar, but significant changes occur nonetheless.

In humans, the stages between birth and adulthood include infancy, childhood (or pre-adolescence), and adolescence. Although these stages are not defined by specific ages or lengths of time, as they vary from individual to individual, they do occur within a specific range of times after birth.

INFANCY

The first two years after birth are generally considered the period of *infancy*. A newborn can be viewed as an organism with great potential. In the two years following birth, significant development and growth occur. By the end of this time, the weight of the baby will have quadrupled, the length will have increased by an average of 30 cm, and maturation of certain body systems will have taken place. Although the extremities grow more rapidly than the trunk, the body retains the big-headed, chubby, short-limbed appearance characteristic of toddlers.

At birth, many organ systems including the gastrointestinal tract, the immune system, and the respiratory system, are still immature and and continue to develop during infancy. Significant maturation of the nervous system also occurs during infancy. Made up of the brain, the spinal cord, and peripheral nerves, the *nervous system* processes information through its basic functional unit, the nerve cell. Brain growth during infancy is very rapid; the brain increases threefold in weight, achieving 70% of its full growth. All the nerve cells in a human are present at birth and do not divide. Instead, the nervous system matures by forming additional nerve fibers which project from the nerve cells. These fibers form increasingly complex connections. This enormous increase in the number of connections between nerve cells result in greater nerve tissue activity. The transmission of signals among nerve cells becomes much more rapid as cellular membranes in the nervous system mature, resulting in the increased capabilities that occur during the juvenile stage of life. While development of the nervous system occurs through a programmed sequence of physiological events, environmental factors also play an important role in this process. Nutrition and sensory stimulation during early life are essential for successful maturation of the nervous system, which is reflected in the changing mental and physical capabilities of the growing infant.

CHILDHOOD

Childhood begins at the end of infancy (two years of age) and ceases about 10 years later, at puberty. During this time the rates of growth are undramatic and continue at a slow but steady pace; the changes in body proportions which occur as a toddler becomes a child are the result of rapid growth of the extremities coupled with a decrease in adipose (fat) tissue and an increase in muscle mass. This produces the long-legged and slender but sturdy child. The gastrointestinal system is fully developed and functional, allowing a child to consume all kinds of foods; control of the sphincter muscles has developed, and so the child can be toilet-trained. The immune system matures during this time, and the circulatory and respiratory systems become fully developed.

Major development of the nervous system is still occurring throughout childhood. The brain reaches its adult size by the age of five. The sequential development of nervous tissue and neural connections allows a child to perform increasingly complex tasks requiring higher levels of gross and fine motor coordination. Such tasks include learning to use language—to comprehend, speak, read, and write it—to use tools and to control behavior. The eyes continue to develop, resulting in changes in visual powers; as the eyeball grows and increases in length and width, vision improves until, at about the age of five, most children have 20/20 vision. If the eyeball grows more in length than in width, the child will be myopic or near-sighted. Another variation in eyeball growth may cause an astigmatism or indistinct vision.

The endocrine and reproductive systems show very little change until late in childhood when profound changes signal the beginning of puberty. As you will see later in this learning experience, hormones are involved in regulating growth and have a profound impact subsequently during adolescence.

ADOLESCENCE

Adolescence is a time of sexual maturation, during which the ability to reproduce is achieved. Adolescence generally occurs between the ages of 10 and 18 for girls and from 12 to 20 for boys. During these ages, many physical changes occur, the result of development of the endocrine and reproductive systems. These changes include a marked increase in growth rate which results in an increase in body size, changes in body shape, and rapid development of the reproductive organs. Nearly every muscular and skeletal dimension of the body is involved in the "growth spurt" at this time—the growth rate during adolescence is nearly twice that of the childhood growth rate. Lengthening of the skeletal structure prior to increasing muscle mass often results in a gangly appearance, especially in boys. Differential growth rates of the extremities may also result in ears that seem to belong to a different head and a nose that

Figure 9.2
Alice in adolescent land.

takes center stage. Overactive glands in the skin result in the bane of the teenage years, acne.

The nervous system continues to fine tune, enabling increasingly more complex motor skills and the development of abstract reasoning. Adolescence is, biologically speaking, a tumultuous time when the body undergoes tremendous change. To the individual experiencing puberty, these changes may seem to be uncoordinated, uncalled for, and unfair; however, the sequence of events during this stage are highly coordinated and regulated and by the end of adolescence will have resulted in a mature adult.

GROWING UP

Growth is achieved by mitosis and cell division; the single fertilized egg must divide to produce hundreds, thousands, millions of cells. The rate of growth, and the final size of the organism, its parts and its organs, are determined by the rate and extent of cell division. The early stages of embryogenesis represent one of the most rapid growth periods in the development of an organism. Cell division is also responsible for growth throughout the life of the organism—increases in organ size, muscle mass, and skeletal length.

Growth after birth in humans slows down to a steady pace until adolescence when the "growth spurt" occurs. Significant increases occur not only in height and weight but also in body parameters such as pelvic and shoulder size, hand and foot length, and head circumference. Figure 9.3 shows a "typical" individual velocity curve of growth. A velocity curve is defined as the rate of growth per year. (Notice that the rate can decline even while size continues to increase.)

A multicellular organism reaches adulthood through a sequence of events. The fact that organisms grow in proportion, and that most reach a predetermined size range, suggests that the growth process—when an organism will grow, how it will grow, and how big it will be—is carefully controlled. Controlling mechanisms determine what information in the DNA will be expressed (differentiation), and when and where in the organism growth will occur.

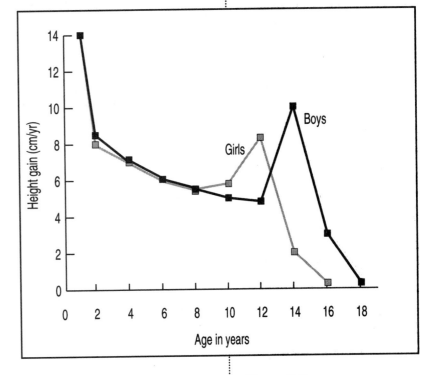

Figure 9.3
Velocity curve for height in boys and girls.

► ANALYSIS

Write responses to the following in your notebook.

1. For the first several weeks after birth, mortality (death) rates can be very high. In some countries, babies may not be named until they have survived this period. Based on the reading, explain the possible reasons for this high rate of death.

2. Many activities such as smoking, drinking alcohol, driving a car, working at jobs requiring motor coordination and strength, and marriage, are only permitted once an individual reaches a particular age, usually between 16 and 21. What do you think needs to happen developmentally before these activities are permissible?

3. What information in the graph shown in Figure 9.3 suggests that growth is regulated?

4. What do you think is responsible for the growth spurt during adolescence shown in Figure 9.3? Why do you think this occurs?

I Won't Grow Up (Without my Hormones)

Infancy is a period of continued rapid growth that, in humans, slows in later childhood. Human infants may grow as much as seven to ten inches in the first year. With this change in size come changes in abilities. The baby is capable of many more activities such as sitting up, crawling, feeding itself, talking, and in some cases, walking. These increasing capabilities reflect the increasing development of the nervous system. In its second year, the baby grows four to five inches. Another significant growth spurt occurs with the onset of puberty and the sex hormone-induced changes of adolescence. The growth rates during the first two years, and again at puberty, are greater than at any other time in post-birth life.

What is it that controls the rate of cell divisions that results in growth? One of the most important factors in controlling growth in organisms is in regulation through growth hormones. What are hormones, anyway? You may have been told that teenagers are ruled by "raging hormones." Yet you feel your life is ruled by you and your thought processes. What do hormones have to do with it?

In a single-celled organism most communication takes place within the cell, or between the cell and its environment across the cell membrane. One of the consequences of being multicellular, however, is that the methods for communicating within an organism become more complex. During embryogenesis communication among neighboring cells signals cells to develop specialized functions and to organize into tissues and organs. In multicellular organisms communication within the organism is required for many reasons; for the organisms to continue to grow and develop; for the organism to maintain temperature and internal balance within an environment that may be changing; for the organism to communicate within itself concerning what different parts are doing and what is happening in its environment.

A multicellular organism communicates internally by using two organ systems: the nervous and the endocrine systems. The nervous system enables a multicellular organism to send messages around the body and to respond to internal and external signals. The nervous system signals hunger, danger, the need for rest and repair, and enables the body to respond to its environment.

The other organ system responsible for internal communication is the *endocrine system*. Made up of seemingly independent organs (*glands*) found throughout the body, the endocrine system produces a remarkable array of chemical substances, *hormones*, which can be either lipids or small proteins, that are responsible for regulating growth and development and maintaining the stability of the body's internal environment. Figure 9.4 shows the glands of the endocrine system. Although widely separated in the body, these glands form an integrated system by producing hormones which can work with other hormones to effect a specific action. An example of this concerted action is seen with the hormones glucocorticoids from the adrenal cortex, thyroxine from the thyroid gland and somatotropin from the pituitary gland that all work together to regulate metabolic activity (breakdown and synthesis of biomolecules) in cells.

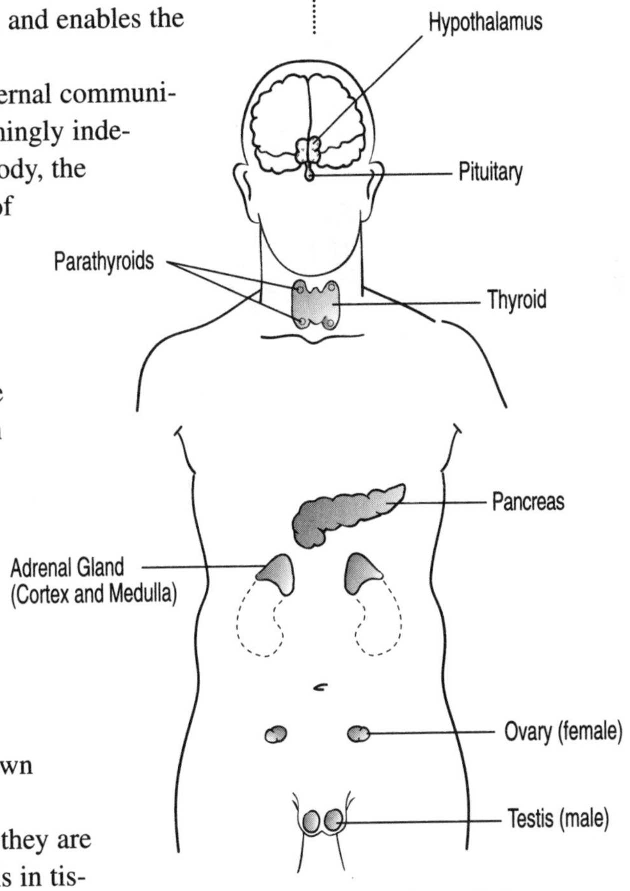

Hormones travel from the gland in which they are produced through the bloodstream to target cells in tissues and regulate the activity of those cells. The human endocrine system can be compared to a radio broadcast system in that it is capable of communicating via a signal with millions of cells (listeners) that may be located at some distance away from the origin of the signal. Just as a radio has a set of filters which allow you (by turning a dial or pushing a button) to choose to receive only certain broadcast frequencies, these target cells have specific proteins on their surfaces called *receptors* which will receive or bind only certain hormones.

Figure 9.4
Endocrine system in humans.

Hormones play vital roles in growth and development in animals; they contribute to the growth of the embryo within the womb, stimulate the body's growth from infancy to adolescence, and stimulate and guide the transformation from adolescent to adult. In insects, juvenile hormones control changes which occur between hatching and adulthood. Amphibian development is also regulated by hormones. In plants, hormones regulate when a plant will flower and fruit, and when the leaves will turn color in autumn.

Certain hormones have the specific function of regulating growth. In most vertebrate animals, growth is regulated by the hormone *somatotropin* (generally referred to as growth hormone) which is produced in the *pituitary gland* located near the base of the brain (see Figure 9.5). This hormone exerts its primary effects on the long bones of the limbs where significant growth occurs. Growth hormone appears to act by binding to receptors on the surface of cells and stimulating the cells to divide. In order to coordinate bodily growth, somatotropin must affect bone and organ growth in a controlled manner.

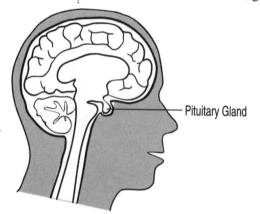

Pituitary Gland

Figure 9.5
Site of the pituitary gland below the brain.

In children, human growth hormone promotes the growth of bones and other tissues. In adults, the hormone helps to maintain bone and muscle mass and enables the body to derive energy from food; late in life the level of growth hormone drops, and this may be responsible for some old-age characteristics such as decrease in muscle mass and bone density, and the accumulation of fat.

In plants, growth hormone will determine how tall a plant may get, its rate of growth, and its direction of growth in response to environmental influences (such as light, gravity, wind direction, and moisture). Plants make different kinds of growth hormone, several of which are made in the apical stem of the plant.

How tall will I be? When will I be full grown? The answer to these questions is determined by several factors: the information in your DNA inherited from our parents, your hormones, and certain external factors such as nutrition. Growth may happen early in some, later in others. There may be a lot of growth or a little, but inevitably for most individuals, growth happens.

▶ ANALYSIS

Write responses to the following questions in your notebook and be prepared to discuss them in class.

1. What roles do hormones play in regulating an organism's growth?

2. How do you think hormones do this?

3. How do hormones move around in the body? Why is it necessary that hormones travel?

4. What might happen to an organism that has no growth-regulating hormones? Why might this be a disadvantage? an advantage?

5. How might the amount of hormones produced affect the survival of an organism? of its offspring?

EXTENDING IDEAS

Physiological development of the central nervous system is influenced by the level of sensory stimulation during infancy. Animal experiments have shown that blindfolding one eye during early life leads to abnormal development of the optic nerve in that eye, and exposure to blue light only during this time leads to an inability to respond to other colors. Young birds, deprived of the learning that normally occurs in early life, fail to develop the neurological capability to follow moving objects. Studies on humans have indicated that lack of sensory stimulation during infancy and early childhood can result in children who are less capable of learning. Research these studies and explain the implications for babies and for early childhood education.

Computer aging techniques allow the determination of how a person might look at later stages of life. This technique has been used extensively in the search for missing children; when a child has been missing for many years the computer aging technique enables investigators to obtain a reasonable approximation of how that child's appearance may have changed over time. Research this technique and explain what features of growth and development are taken into consideration. (One magazine article that describes this technique is "The Child Finders Blend High Tech and High Purpose," by Donald Dale Jackson, *Smithsonian*, October 1995, vol. 26, no. 7, pp. 70–80.)

When Althea was 18 months old she was given a peanut butter sandwich by her mother. Instead of reacting with delight, she reacted violently; her face began to swell, her blood pressure dropped and she struggled to breathe. For some children, eating a peanut butter sandwich—the mainstay of childhood—can be a life-threatening experience. In the last decade, the number of children allergic to peanuts has doubled and the rate of peanut allergy appears to be increasing. Some researchers believe that this and other food allergies are the result of exposure of young children to certain foods before their immune systems are mature (usually between the ages of two and three). Research allergies to certain foods such as milk, eggs, peanuts, strawberries, and determine what is understood about the relationship between the immune system and early exposure to these foods.

ON THE JOB

PLANT PATHOLOGIST   Do you have a strong interest in keeping plants healthy? Plant pathologists are scientists who study the diseases of plants and specialize in keeping plants healthy. This means identifying the living agents which cause the disease, as well as nonliving agents such as air pollutants, or other environmental factors. New diseases and changes in known agents remain a constant threat to forests, crops and landscape plants. The interaction between plants and causative agents can be studied at the molecular level, or the organismal level, or within an ecosystem. Plant pathologists work in laboratories and with plant breeders to identify techniques for managing plant diseases in ways that are safe for the environment and for consumers. The laboratory techniques and procedures used by plant pathologists are the techniques and tools used by microbiologists, crop scientists, soil scientists, geneticists, ecologists, and molecular biologists. With a four year college degree, positions as research assistants are available. Or, the expertise can be used in working as greenhouse managers, park and golf course superintendents, and salespersons in agribusiness. With a master's or doctoral degree plant pathologists can teach in a university or pursue independent research in a university or other laboratory. Classes such as biology, chemistry, ecology, math, English, and computer science are recommended.

ATHLETIC TRAINER   Do you like sports? Are you interested in health and fitness? Athletic trainers are involved in many stages of helping athletes achieve top performances. They are responsible for advising coaches and players on how to prevent injuries. When injuries occur on the field or court they are there to administer first aid and are responsible for follow-up care such as water therapy, rehabilitation exercise, and any continued treatment prescribed by the athlete's physician. Athletic trainers are also involved in educating students, parents, and coaches in safe practices for playing sports and taking care of their bodies through proper exercise and diet prior to athletic events. Educational requirements for becoming a trainer include a four-year college degree with a major in anatomy and physiology or exercise physiology and/or a master's degree in athletic training. Trainers need to be certified by the National Athletic Trainers Association and licensed in their respective states.

Puberty: The Metamorphosis to Maturity

PROLOGUE In the last learning experience, you focused on the period of development and growth that characterizes young organisms as they increase in size, and on the action of growth hormones that guide this process. The transition time between the end of childhood and the beginning of adulthood is referred to as adolescence, a term encompassing the full range of the biological, psychological, and social developments. In general, adolescence in girls spans the ages between ten and eighteen; in boys, from twelve to twenty.

Humans become sexually mature and capable of reproduction during the period of adolescence called *puberty*. The age at which an individual "enters" puberty varies from individual to individual. External factors, such as general nutritional health, may be involved as well as family history (inherited characteristics). In girls, the onset of puberty is marked by the beginning of menstruation (the menarche); in boys, by a growth spurt. Further changes, such as the development of secondary sex characteristics, happen around the same time. What initiates such dramatic changes in a juvenile's body? Why does it happen when it does? Why does puberty occur?

Setting the Stage for Adulthood

INTRODUCTION The sequence of events during development can be shown most clearly with graphs. The following graphs indicate when specific events of puberty and adolescence take place.

► TASK

Study Figures 10.1 and 10.2 which show the sequence of visible indications of puberty, collectively referred to as *secondary sex characteristics*. (The *primary sex characteristic* is the gonad—testes or ovaries—which determines gender.) Working with your partner discuss the following and write responses in your notebook:

1. Identify the changes that occur during puberty for boys and for girls.

2. Describe the meaning of "variability of onset."

3. Identify any factors that might influence the timing of the onset of puberty.

4. Compare the two graphs. What conclusions can you make from this comparison?

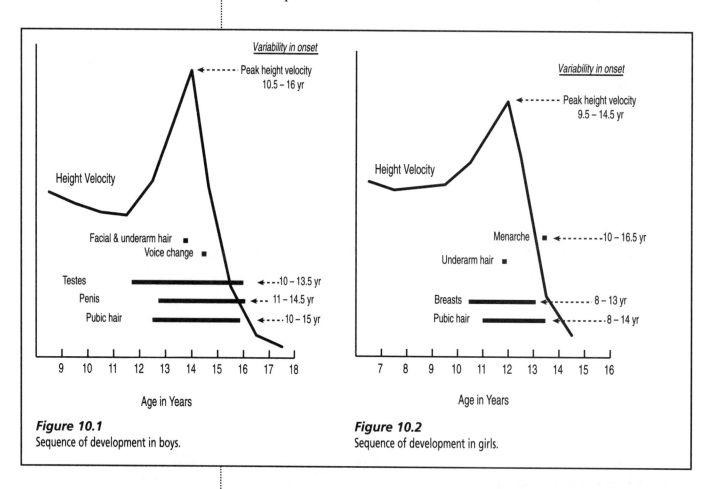

Figure 10.1
Sequence of development in boys.

Figure 10.2
Sequence of development in girls.

► ANALYSIS

Write an essay about your current stage of life. Your essay should include a description of the sequence of events in (male or female) puberty, how puberty is similar or different in males and females, and the significance of these differences. Speculate on what you think might cause these changes to occur and the reasons they happen.

What's Happening?

DEVELOPING AN IDENTITY

During the first six weeks of human embryonic development, it is difficult to tell the girls from the boys. Structurally and biochemically, the male and female embryos are identical. However, a quick peek into their genes would reveal the difference (a difference in the sex chromosomes). The difference becomes visibly obvious when undifferentiated tissues begin to develop into the gonads (ovaries or testes) in the lower abdomen. The same tissues in the embryo are thought to give rise to male or female reproductive organs.

In the seventh week of development, in male embryos these tissues begin to produce male hormones called *androgens*, especially one called *testosterone*. Testosterone stimulates the development of male genitalia and organs of the male reproductive tract. In the absence of androgens, female embryos develop ovaries which start to produce the hormone called *estrogen*; the embryo then develops other female reproductive organs.

WHY NOW?

Before puberty, girls and boys have about the same proportions of muscle mass, skeletal mass, and body fat. By the end of puberty, women have twice as much body fat as men, whereas men have 1.5 times the skeletal and muscle mass of women. What controls these changes during puberty? The pituitary gland is a major endocrine structure involved in the cascade of hormones that streams through the body during puberty. Located beneath and controlled by the hypothalamus region of the brain, the pituitary gland produces many different hormones. When stimulated by luteinizing hormone releasing factor (LRF) from the hypothalamus, the anterior lobe of the pituitary produces the follicle-stimulating hormone (FSH) and luteinizing hormone (LH) that initiate changes during puberty.

FSH and LH act on the gonads; FSH is involved in sperm production in the male and stimulates egg-producing follicles to grow and develop in the ovary of the female. In males, LH stimulates cells in the testes to produce testosterone whereas, in the female, LH stimulates follicles to release eggs. The joint action of LH and FSH cause the follicles of the ovary to secrete estrogen. Figure 10.3 (on the next page) shows the cascade of hormone production and the changes in the hormone levels from the juvenile stage to the adult stage.

Testosterone and estrogen are involved in the production of sperm

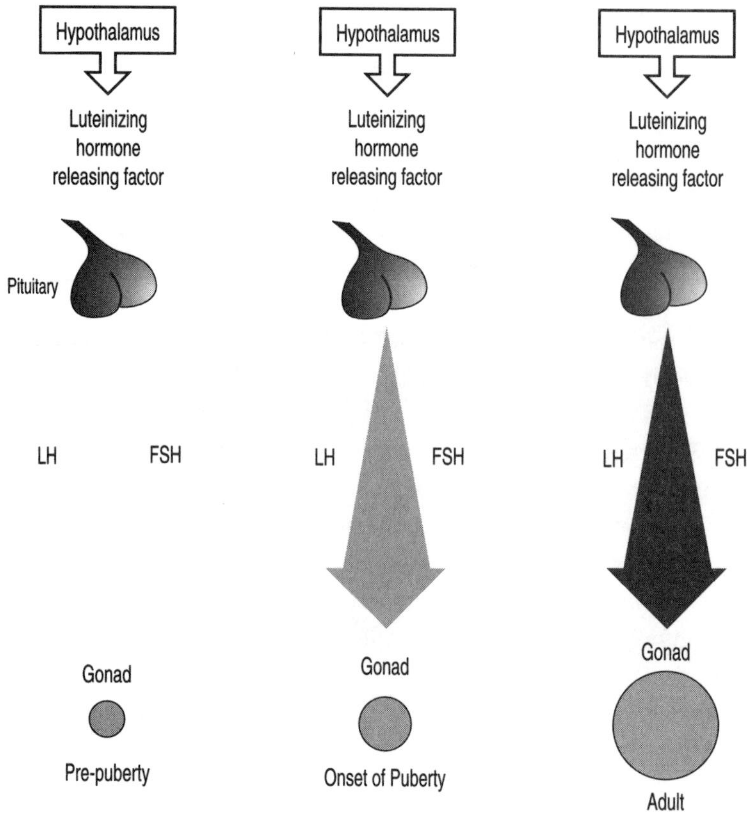

Figure 10.3
Hormones involved in the onset of puberty. The production of luteinizing hormone (LH) and follicle-stimulating hormone (FSH).

and egg respectively and are also responsible for the appearance of secondary sex characteristics that marks the change from the juvenile stage to the sexually mature adult. In males, the testosterone produced by the testes (and in small amounts by the adrenal glands) is the main male hormone of puberty and adulthood. Testosterone targets many kinds of cells in the body and is involved in the maturation of the penis, the maintenance of the testes and the reproductive tract, sperm production, changes in the larynx, patterns of body hair, patterns of behavior, and general body configuration. Testosterone also stimulates muscle development. The testosterone molecule, a shortened version of the cholesterol molecule, is one of the organic compounds known as *steroids*. Males also secrete small amounts of estrogen.

In females, estrogen, produced by the ovaries, is the principal female hormone. Like testosterone, estrogen is also a steroid that binds to many kinds of cells in the body. Estrogen stimulates the development of breasts, the widening of hips, maturation of the reproductive tract allowing for the ability to bear children, and changes in patterns of body hair. Secretion of estrogen causes the maturation and maintenance of the ovaries and the reproductive tract. Figure 10.4 summarizes the interactions that result in the production of estrogen and testosterone. Females also secrete a small amount of testosterone, produced by the adrenal glands, which regulates pubic and axillary hair development.

Along with estrogen, LH and FSH are responsible for stimulating and maintaining the *menstrual cycle*. During that cycle, an ovum (egg) is produced and released approximately once every twenty-eight days. Other hormones cause the thickening and increased blood supply of the uterine lining in preparation for receiving the fertilized egg. If the egg is not fertilized, the uterus sheds its lining (referred to as menstrual fluid), and the cycle begins again. These cycles of egg production and shedding continue for approximately forty years at which time hormonal production slows and ovulation ceases (menopause).

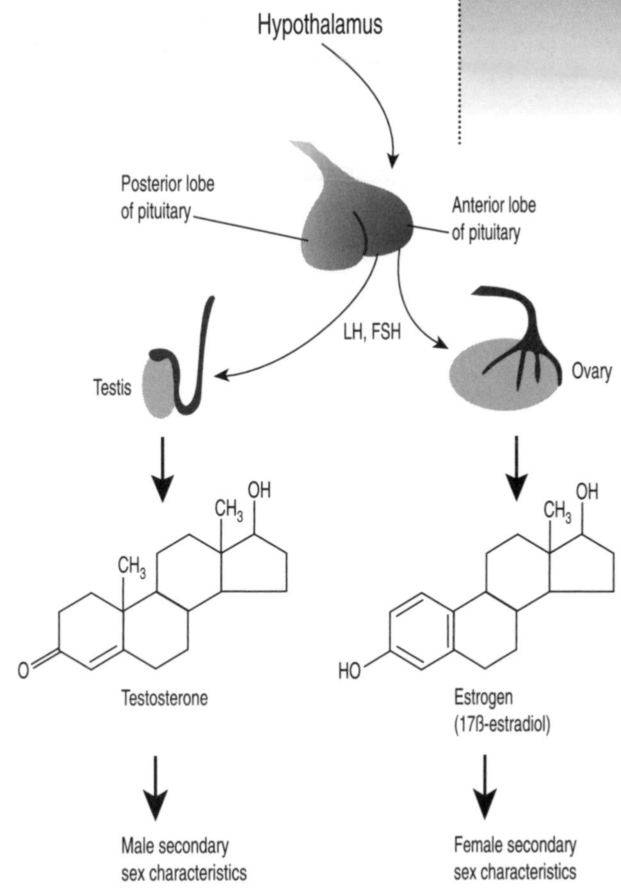

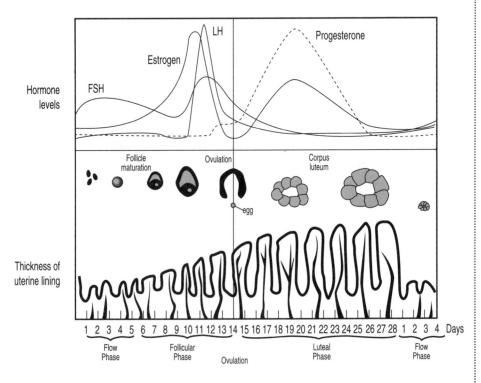

Figure 10.4
Hypothalamus-pituitary-gonad interaction in human puberty.

Figure 10.5
Hormone levels in the three phases of the menstrual cycle.

Puberty can be considered analogous to metamorphosis which marks the transition from the juvenile to adult stage in insects and amphibians and is also controlled by hormones. In Alice's *Adventures in Wonderland*, written by Lewis Carroll, Alice complains to the Caterpillar that she is very confused by the changes in size she has undergone. The Caterpillar finds nothing confusing about it at all.

> *"Well, perhaps you haven't found it so yet," said Alice, "but when you have to turn into a chrysalis—you will some day, you know—and then after that into a butterfly, I should think you'll feel it a little bit queer, won't you?"*
> *"Not a bit," said the Caterpillar.*
> *"Well, perhaps your feelings may be different," said Alice, "all I know is it would feel very queer to me."*

▶ ANALYSIS

Write responses to the following in your notebook.

1. What biological events cause the onset of puberty? Refer to Figures 10.3 and 10.4 to help you in your explanation.

2. Explain the various ways that puberty correlates with reproductive readiness.

3. Examine Figure 10.5:
   a. What information does this graph tell you?
   b. How does this information relate to concepts in the reading?

MAKING DECISIONS

What problems and choices confront teenage athletes, dancers, and students in their quest for excellence and perfection? The following reading "Teen Choices" discusses anorexia, bulimia, and steroid use as consequences of this quest. Be prepared to discuss these and other ideas in class that have been presented in the reading.

• What are the social pressures from one's peers?
• What are adult expectations?
• What distinguishes dieting from anorexia?
• What are the biological consequences of these disorders?
• How might those trapped in these cycles be helped?

▶ TEEN CHOICES

When Christy Henrich died in 1994 at the age of 22, she weighed only 61 pounds. How could this happen to a world class gymnast? In 1988, she had narrowly missed being named to the United States Olympic team. When a gymnast judge told her she was "fat," although she then weighed only 95 pounds, she became obsessed about losing weight. Her eating habits became so extreme that finally she was eating only an apple a day, then only an apple slice a day, all the while training for hours in the gym.

Christy had become the victim of two eating disorders: *anorexia nervosa*, a form of self-starvation, and *bulimia nervosa*, characterized by binge eating followed by vomiting and/or the use of laxatives. Although Christy was hospitalized in 1993 when her weight fell to 52 pounds, and gained back some weight in the hospital, the year of starvation had already caused destruction of muscle—including her heart muscle—and organ shrinkage. Her body finally gave out.

It is too simplistic to accept the official cause of Christy's death as "multiple organ failure." The pressures that many gymnasts, ballet dancers, and models feel to be unrealistically thin must also play a causal role. But is this a problem with teenagers and adults who do not have these athletic and professional pressures? Statistics show that 1 in 100 women are anorexic; however, the majority of anorexics are girls between the ages of 12 and 18 and, therefore, the frequency is actually much greater in that age group than in the general population. (About five percent of all anorexics are men.)

ANOREXIA NERVOSA

In this serious physiological and psychological disease, a change in eating patterns results in the body weight being about 20 percent below the expected weight for a healthy person of the same age and height. The anorexic refuses to maintain a healthful body weight, is generally afraid to gain weight, and has a distorted perception of her body size or shape. Studying her image in the mirror, the anorexic sees a fat person, even if she is seriously underweight.

As in the case of Christy Henrich, the effects of anorexia nervosa may be severe and irreversible. External changes are emaciation, dry skin, hair loss and the growth of fine body hair. Internal changes include the cessation of the menstrual cycle (amenorrhea), infertility, low blood pressure, edemic (water retention) swelling, loss in bone density, liver damage, dental problems, cramps, diarrhea, and heart irregularities.

Anorexia nervosa is a growing disorder in our weight-conscious society. Exploring the underlying causes is key to successful recovery and to helping women avoid the illness altogether. A common reason that older people become anorexic, for example, is because of depression. For a teenager, the most obvious and superficial cause may be the desire to be accepted, popular, and wear stylish clothes, but the deeper, subconscious causes may not even be realized. These may include the need to be perfect and to feel control over life, undefined feelings of being powerless, a need for attention and admiration on having self-control, and deep emotional conflicts that often arise from family issues. As a child develops into an adolescent her hips begin to widen and fat is deposited in places where it never was before, at just the time when appearance seems to be most important; so, she begins a diet that becomes uncontrollable.

BULIMIA NERVOSA

Bulimia is characterized by binge eating followed by inappropriate methods to prevent weight gain such as self-induced vomiting or abuse of laxatives. If such behavior occurs at least twice a week for three months, it is classified as bulimia. The type of food consumed during binges varies, but typically it includes sweet, high-calorie foods such as ice cream and other desserts. Binge eating and the resulting purging generally occur in secret amid feelings of loss of control.

The physical effects on the bulimic include: fluid and electrolyte (mineral) abnormalities which may, in turn, lead to heart problems; significant loss of dental enamel and increase in cavities; menstrual irregularities; and metabolic disorders resulting from the loss of stomach acid.

Individuals with bulimia nervosa place an excessive emphasis on body shape and weight, and these features become the most important ones in measuring self-esteem. Compulsive exercising to compensate for the binge eating and to achieve the desired shape and weight often occurs. Statistics show that from one to three percent of adolescent and young adult females are bulimic. The rate of occurrence in males is approximately one-tenth that in females, and the disorder is primarily found in whites.

ANABOLIC STEROIDS

Steroids actually include many lipids in the body, such as testosterone, estrogen, hormones made in the adrenal glands, and cholesterol. However, the statement that someone is "taking steroids" refers, in general, to the use of sex hormones which stimulate secondary sexual characteristics, especially muscle size.

When steroids are present in excess amounts, as in the case of steroid use by athletes, the results can be startling. Steroids can increase muscle mass significantly, increase muscle strength, and improve muscle definition, resulting in a faster, stronger, more durable athlete.

But using steroids is also dangerous. They can stop the growth of long bones, an important determinant of future height. They can also cause testicle shrinkage, liver tumors, abnormal liver metabolism, alterations in tendons, and increase in total cholesterol. Behavioral abnormalities often occur, including excessive irritability, hostility, and mood swings. Steroid use may also provoke anger, distractibility, violent feelings, insomnia, confusion, forgetfulness, and headaches. Before taking steroids, athletes, both professional and amateur, must weigh the trade-offs and the consequences of enhancing performance by this method.

There has been a dramatic rise in steroid use throughout the world. It is a complex problem with social, physiological, psychological, economic, and political variables.

Just how many American teenagers are taking steroids? Although it is difficult to obtain accurate numbers, a University of Michigan study, released in December 1994, reported that more than 200,000 high school males took steroids during that year. Other estimates range as high as 500,000 teens a year with confirmed reports of some starting as early as 10 years of age. At the high school level, teens may get mixed messages from some adults about the importance of muscle mass. After teammates and friends, coaches and teachers ranked second as the source for these mostly illegal drugs.

EXTENDING IDEAS

Hormones play many roles in the body; in addition to physical effects, hormones appear to be involved in influencing social behavior. Oxytocin and vasopressin are two such hormones. Similar in structure and produced by the posterior pituitary gland, these two polypeptides seem to be involved in producing monogamous and maternal (in females) and paternal (in males) behavior. These effects are described engagingly in "What Makes a Parent Put up With It All?" by Natalie Angier in *The Beauty of the Beastly,* Houghton Mifflin Co., NY, 1995, p. 27. Research these hormones and determine their structures, sites of action, and roles in influencing behavior.

ON THE JOB

DEVELOPMENTAL PSYCHOLOGIST   Developmental psychologists study the development of people from birth through old age—including their behavior, their capacities and their needs. Psychologists usually concentrate in one specialty, such as developmental psychology. Their work often takes place in day care centers, preschools, hospitals or clinics. A counseling psychologist may work with people to help solve problems or to make decisions. School psychologists' work is often in preventive or developmental psychology. Psychologists get to know people through methods such as interviewing or observing, testing or personal histories. Psychologists work in a variety of settings ranging from health care facilities, to social service organizations, to management consulting firms, to market research firms, to schools or universities. Some psychologists have private practices. Psychologists have a doctorate in psychology, but are not medical doctors and cannot prescribe medications. Classes such as English, math, science, and foreign languages (French and German) are useful.

...GROWN!

PROLOGUE **W**hat controls growth? We return to that question in this learning experience. For the last few days, you have been exploring hormones that affect growth and development of organisms. In this learning experience, you will complete the experiment you began in Learning Experience 9 and apply your knowledge about growth and the observations from your experiment to analyze your experimental results and to reach a conclusion about the role of hormones in the regulation (control) of the growth of organisms.

DID MY INVESTMENT GROW?

INTRODUCTION This is the final analysis of the Learning Experience 9 investigation "Will My Investment Grow?" in which you determined the effects of an unknown compound on pea plants. Were the company's claims accurate? Did the compound affect how the plants grew? How? After your group has analyzed the results of the experiment, identify what factors have been affecting growth in these plants. As you reach your conclusions, you will need to apply your knowledge of growth and development from the module.

▶ TASK

1. Read through the entire Task before compiling your laboratory report.

2. With your group, determine how you will analyze your data. Discuss the meaning of the results and the conclusions that you can draw from them. (Be sure to take notes on the group discussion to use in writing the laboratory report.) Your laboratory report should contain the following information:
    *   the purpose of the experiment (that is, the scientific question being addressed)
    *   your hypothesis

- the protocol your group used for the experiment, including materials and procedure
- the raw data (the numbers as recorded each day)
- a graph of growth curves
- analysis of the data (including growth rate (cm/day))
- possible sources of error
- discussion about the way this product might affect plants and why it might have affected short and tall plants differently
  - Did the growth compound have any effect on the plants?
  - If so, which plant(s) benefited most significantly from the growth compound? How would you demonstrate that from your data?
  - How might you explain the difference?
- conclusions about the effectiveness of this product as a growth promoter, including your conclusions about the veracity (truthfulness) of the biotechnology company's claims
- recommendation of the product as an investment potential including:
  - why a company might wish to develop a product that would help plants grow taller
  - your decision about whether or not to recommend this product

3. Read "Shoot to Root, Are You There?" as support material for use in the conclusion section of your report. Based on this article, can you identify the product of this biotechnology company?

READING

Shoot to Root, Are You There?

Like all multicellular organisms, plants need to communicate. To be well formed and to function effectively, each part of the plant must be in communication with the other parts. Otherwise, the plant would be incapable of carrying out its life functions such as growth.

Plant growth is indeterminate; that is, unlike many organisms whose size ranges are fixed by heredity, there are no absolute restrictions on the precise size a plant may reach or the precise shape it might assume. But growth is not random. Plants produce predictable structures and patterns that are characteristic of each species, indicating that plant growth is regulated. The controls on growth rate and the patterns of growth ensure that a plant will grow in a coordinated fashion. In addition, these controls enable a plant to respond to environmental conditions—light, gravity, wind direction and moisture—which are essential for an organism that cannot move to different locations. As in other organisms, the controlling factors are hormones.

Evidence that plants contain hormones was first suggested in experiments by Charles Darwin and his son Francis in the late 1880s. It was a common observation that plants curve toward the sun or other source of light (*phototropism*). When the Darwins covered the tip of a growing plant with an opaque barrier, the plant no longer bent toward the light. This suggested to the Darwins that some influence from the tip, probably a chemical substance, caused one side of the plant to grow faster than the other side of the plant, causing curvature. This hypothesis was greeted with skepticism by other plant scientists, largely because Darwin (while known for his theory of evolution) was not recognized as a plant biologist. In that field, he was considered an outsider.

Fifty years passed before Frits Went (a plant biologist) carried out the definitive experiment to prove the existence of this chemical substance. Went removed the tip of a plant and placed it on an agar block for several hours. He then placed the agar block back on the plant, but this time on one side of the stem, and placed the plant in the dark. Even in the dark, the stem began to move away from the block as if it were responding to a light source on the side away from the block (see Figure 11.1).

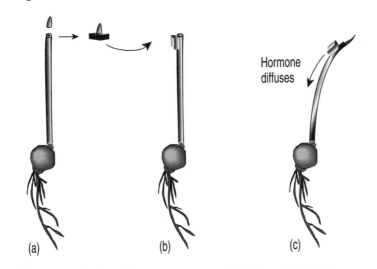

Hormone diffuses

(a) (b) (c)

Figure 11.1
The Went Experiment
(a) The growing tip of the plant is removed and placed on an agar block for several hours. (b) The agar block is then placed on one side of the plant from which the tip has been removed. (c) The plant is placed in the dark and the response is observed.

Went's experiment demonstrated that a diffusible substance (a substance able to move through the agar block) able to stimulate growth was present in the tip of a plant. This substance stimulated cell growth in the cells on the side of the plant next to the block, causing this side of the plant to grow faster than the other side and inducing a curvature of the plant. Subsequently this chemical substance was identified as indole acetic acid, or auxin, which seems to promote growth by causing cells to elongate.

In the late nineteenth century, Japanese rice farmers noted extraordinarily tall seedlings rising out of their fields of otherwise uniform plants. Hoping that these tall plants might result in a strain of giant rice, the farmers tended the tall plants carefully only to find that they died before flowering. Many years later, scientists discovered that the source of this tall growth was actually an infection of the rice plants by a fungus which produced a substance they called *gibberellic acid*. Since then, gibberellic acid has been found in many plants. It stimulates plants to grow taller by causing stem elongation. Another attempt to use gibberellic acid for improving crop production was in the cereal industry. It was hoped that by applying tiny quantities of this hormone to cereal and grass crops, farmers might accelerate crop growth and obtain greater yields at harvest. The results of this have been disappointing: while gibberellic acid does promote growth during early development, later on the untreated plants catch up with the gibberellic acid treated plants, so that both groups ultimately reach the same size and, therefore, result in similar crop yields.

Since these first experiments, many plant hormones have been identified. Hormones are involved in seed germination, growth, flowering, reproduction, and aging of plants; they play a role in the ability of seeds to remain dormant for long periods of time. In both plants and animals, hormones play a variety of different but essential roles in the growth, development, and maintenance of the organism.

DOES GROWTH HORMONE WORK?

In recent years, human growth hormone has been manufactured using techniques of genetic engineering. The compound is available by prescription. This availability has raised some issues which are addressed in the article "Are Short Kids Sick?" that follows.

After you have read the article, you are asked to respond to "Lawrence," a friend who is asking your advice about receiving growth hormone treatments. As you read the article, take notes on:
- how growth hormones work
- the results of the experiment
- economic issues
- other factors involved in your decision

Are Short Kids 'Sick'?

by Rick Weiss, Washington Post, March 15, 1994.

It seemed like the perfect drug for America, where "standing tall" is synonymous with success: a genetically engineered hormone that adds inches to children whose growth is lagging.

Human growth hormone, a laboratory-produced knockoff of a naturally occurring brain chemical, was approved nine years ago by the Food and Drug Administration as a growth-spurring medicine for those few children who fail to make the hormone on their own. But increasingly the drug is being used by children for whom it was never intended and may not work, spawning concerns that the drug's makers and distributors are overpromoting the hormone to expand the lucrative market. The issue is also rekindling a broader debate over the ethics of using biotechnology to change physical traits.

Only about 7,000 children in the United States suffer from classical growth hormone deficiency, a syndrome that can leave them four feet tall as adults. Yet the drug has become the country's 43rd-largest-selling pharmaceutical, according to Med Ad News, a trade publication, and is now being used by an estimated 20,000 to 25,000 children.

When seeking permission to market the drug, the U.S. manufacturers, Genentech and Eli Lilly, and their licensed suppliers assured the FDA they would work to limit the medicine's distribution to those who are truly growth-hormone-deficient. Indeed, said Robert Huizenga, a Beverly Hills internist who has closely followed the drug's evolution, "for a long time, only pediatric endocrinologists could get it for growth-deficient kids. There was this incredible restriction." But lately, he said, the supply has eased. "Now the Genentech representatives are saying anybody can get it. I could prescribe it for athletes or anybody I want and I really don't think anybody would ask any questions," he said.

Jim Weiss, a spokesman for Genentech, said that although any doctor can write a prescription for the drug, the vast majority of prescriptions are written by pediatric endocrinologists. "We have strictly marketed it and made it available to that group," he said.

He added that much of the drug's increase in sales could be attributed to improved vigilance by doctors and parents to identify children with growth hormone deficiencies. He said there were apparently more such children than doctors had presumed, and he denied that the company was pitching the drug more actively. "Ultimately it's the doctor who writes the prescription, based on their best judgment," he said. "From our perspective we have marketed this drug responsibly."

...Industry observers have worried from the start that the drug, which costs $10,000 to $20,000 or more a year, might get prescribed for children who are short for reasons other than hormone deficiency—or even for medium-sized kids—even though it has not been shown to add to these children's final height. Concerns about the potential for abuse rose last week with the expiration of a seven-year marketing monopoly held by Genentech and Lilly. Three other companies are prepared to enter the market, and experts expect the competition to prompt a drop in prices and increase access to the drug. Already, the hormone has found a black-market following among high school and professional athletes as a body-building drug. The fear is that a combination of aggressive marketing practices and cheaper and easier

Continued on next page

access to the drug could soon add up to a major problem of overuse.

The situation is complicated because new methods of testing for growth hormone production show that the term "deficiency" can be open to interpretation. Indeed, said Brian Stabler, a professor of psychology and pediatrics at the University of North Carolina, the old definition of growth hormone deficiency had been rather arbitrary. Now, he said, "nobody in pediatric endocrinology has agreed on what the cutoff of normal should be."

At the same time, preliminary studies suggest that the hormone may in fact be a useful treatment for more growth conditions than had originally been assumed. In one unexpected application, it clearly adds to the final height of children who are short due to chronic kidney disease. It even speeds growth in some short children who do not fit anyone's definition of having a growth hormone deficiency. But it will be years before doctors know for certain whether these children actually end up taller than they would have or if they are simply reaching their adult height a little bit sooner. Long-term side effects of hormone supplements for these children, if there are any, may not show up for years.

Some parents aren't waiting to find out. Robert and Annette Bursley of Collins, Ohio, had their preschooler David checked out when it became clear to them he was not growing as fast as his peers. Tests showed he was not deficient in growth hormone, and doctors presumed his short stature was a family trait (his father is 5-10; his mother is 5-1). With a predicted final height of less than five feet, his doctor offered the possibility of growth hormone shots.

"It was a hard decision to make," said his mother, who was concerned that the combination of her son being very short and also having a mild speech disorder might cause him problems as an adult. "I was so worried about his being extremely short and it being hard to get a job, we went ahead and did it." Her insurance from work has paid the bills of more than $30,000 per year.

Now, at age 14, after taking six shots a week for more than six years, David is 4-10 and growing at a rate just below average for his age. No one can say for sure if he would have grown that much anyway—many children get a late start growing. But his parents are convinced he's taller than he would have been without the hormone, and plan to continue treatment for a few more years. "We're thrilled," his mother said.

A CALL FOR RESTRICTIONS

...Whatever the fate of human growth hormone, experts said, the debate is a harbinger of dilemmas to come as biotechnology produces new drugs that can alter the body's growth, development and appearance. At issue are difficult questions about looking or being different from one's peers and the extent to which individuals and society are willing to mold themselves to a particular vision of "normal." In the case of height, everyone agrees that growth hormone should be made available to children who make virtually no growth hormone and are destined to be extremely short. But nobody seems to agree on where to draw the line on who else should be treated.

"The question is going to be, 'How healthy is healthy enough?'" said John Lantos, a professor of pediatrics at the University of Chicago Pritzker School of Medicine. "There is a whole industry of psycho-statural studies funded mostly by the drug companies to document problems in school and problems in self-esteem and to target our hearts as well as our minds to show us that shortness is a real disease.

But how bad a self-esteem problem do kids with big noses have? We could probably show that, so maybe we should be getting them all nose jobs."

…"It's a very political issue," he said. "I feel the debate should focus on at what height shortness is a real problem. I think for a male, 5-5 or 5-6 is the cutoff. Someone 5-7 might wish he were taller, but it's not really a big problem."

PROMISING SCIENCE

…Some doctors said that even if growth hormone only speeds up growth in slow-growing children without adding inches to their final height, it could be worth the expense and hassle of the injections. Stabler of North Carolina said studies have shown that many of the behavioral problems that go along with short stature can be alleviated with growth hormone treatments, apparently because the children are able to avoid the stigma of being short during those childhood years when they are most sensitive to being teased.

But that is exactly the line that some believe marks the beginning of dangerous territory, in which medicine is used to deal with what is essentially a social problem.

They say teachers and parents should be helping kids to accept themselves as they are, rather than giving them drugs to make them "better." "As we use [growth hormone] in more and more children and see that it may be working, it affects our ideas about what we want for our children," said Wisconsin's Wyatt.

Some are more vehement. "I think this short stature stuff is just a load of crap to drum up business," said Anne Fausto-Sterling, a professor of medical science at Brown University who has followed growth hormone's rise in popularity with increasing dismay. "I've watched this drug and this story work its way through the regulatory system and watched us invent a disease state in people who are perfectly healthy."

Fausto-Sterling said she is especially concerned about the sexist assumptions implicit in the informal decision by many U.S. doctors to treat boys with projected adult heights of less than 5 feet 2 inches and girls with projected final heights of 4 feet 10 inches. "Here we are making up what's normal and what isn't, we're literally rebuilding the curve of height distribution, and what do we decide but that girls to be normal should be shorter than

---

HUMAN GROWTH HORMONE AT A GLANCE

Hormones are compounds that are secreted by glands in the body and transported by the blood to distant targets. Human growth hormone is secreted by the pituitary gland near the base of the brain. It has a range of positive effects on growth, development and metabolism.

In children, human growth hormone prompts the growth of bones and other tissues; children who can't make the hormone typically reach an adult height of between four and five feet. In adulthood, the hormone helps maintain bone and muscle mass and helps the body derive energy from food; tapering levels during the final decades of life are probably responsible for some of the hallmarks of aging, such as the drop in muscle and bone density and an accumulation of fat.

The human growth hormone that is available as a drug by prescription is virtually identical to the hormone made by the body. In the United States, it is mass-produced in pharmaceutical company laboratories by genetically engineered bacteria that contain copies of a gene for human growth hormone. The hormone is typically injected three times a week into the thigh with a tiny syringe.

boys," she said.

Wisconsin's Wyatt echoed Fausto-Sterling's concern. In the U.S., he said, "short girls are petite. Short boys are shrimps."

Gary Coleman, the actor who appears on one of the Human Growth Foundation's public service announcements, said he'd be concerned if it became too difficult for parents to get human growth hormone for their very short children. He said his doctor has told him that had the drug been available when the actor was growing up, he could be six or even 12 inches taller today....

▶ ANALYSIS

DEAR LAWRENCE, YOU (SHOULD) (SHOULD NOT) GET THOSE INJECTIONS

A very good friend of yours has written to you asking your advice. You have known Lawrence since pre-school and, even though he moved away in sixth grade, you have kept in touch and still consider him a good friend. He is funny, bright, and thoughtful about other people's feelings and needs. He is also very short and very sensitive about this physical feature. Recently Lawrence's doctor suggested that he get growth hormone shots, and he doesn't know what to do. He has written to you for information and advice. From his letter, you can tell that he knows nothing about growth hormone or whether or not it might help.

In a letter, tell Lawrence how you view the situation based on your reading of the article. Include the following items so that Lawrence can use the information and your advice to make his own decision.

- Explain how growth hormone works.

- Analyze the uses of growth hormone as described in the article.

- Mention the economic factors that might affect Lawrence's decision.

- Include any other factors that you would like Lawrence to take into consideration before he makes his decision, such as:
  - Would you recommend that he have any tests done?
  - Would you like him to think about why he thinks it is important to be taller?
  - What other data or information do you think would help Lawrence to make his decision?

Conclude your letter by telling Lawrence what you would do if you were in his place and why you would do it.

▶ Regular supplementation of a cow's diet with small doses of a bovine growth hormone (bovine somatotropin) has been shown to increase milk production by 10–25%. Controversy has arisen as to whether or not the use of a growth hormone to animals used in food production poses a health risk to humans. Obtain literature from groups that hold opposing views (such as the American Dairy Association and the Cancer Prevention Coalition), analyze their presentation of the information, and decide with whom you agree, and why.

ON THE JOB

ENDOCRINOLOGIST Would you like to study hormones that regulate and control body functions? Endocrinologists study hormones, including how they are made, stored, released, degraded, and excreted, and how all these processes are regulated. Endocrinology is an interdisciplinary field concerned with the circulation and local actions of hormones and their role in both health and disease. Hormones are secreted by the endocrine glands and are the substances which regulate the body's reproductive capabilities, growth and development, response to the environment and the provision of energy and nutrients needed for cell function. These natural chemicals increase the body's efficiency, regulate hunger and thirst, digestion, and circulation of the blood. Endocrinologists usually are either involved in research or clinical applications which may include environmental physiology, toxicology, entomology, or animal science. Research includes developing and providing treatment for a wide range of functions and disorders of the human body, including hormone imbalances, metabolism, glandular cancers, dwarfism, and others. Clinical endocrinology includes diagnosing and correcting disorders which arise when the systems malfunction. Endocrinologists may work in private practice, in the pharmaceutical industry, at universities, or for government agencies such as the National Institute of Health, or the U.S. Department of Agriculture. Those in the pharmaceutical industry have training in a variety of biomedical science areas such as physiology, pharmacology, anatomy, zoology and biochemistry. Endocrinologists are medical doctors who have completed a four year college degree, oftentimes in a scientific discipline, four years of medical school, an internship and residency. Classes such as biology, chemistry, English, math, and computer science are useful.

MANY YEARS FROM NOW

PROLOGUE   What is life like after adolescence? What does it mean to be an adult, to age, and to grow old? Following the completion of growth and the attainment of reproductive maturity, changes occur which indicate that an individual is no longer in his or her "first bloom." These changes are gradual, but are they inevitable? If the causes were understood, could these changes be averted? Would we want to stop the aging process?

The quest for eternal youth is a theme that pervades art, literature, philosophy, behavior, and even the history of the world. A conviction that the "fountain of youth" could be found in the New World led the Spanish explorer Ponce de Leon to Florida in the fifteenth century. To this day, that conviction still leads many senior citizens to Florida. Why is there this thirst for youth? Is aging the inevitable and irreversible outcome of growth and development? Is eternal youth desirable? In this learning experience, you will explore what is known about aging; which organisms do it; how humans deal with it; what current theories suggest about how it occurs. Using these concepts, you will decide whether aging is a process that should be controlled or "cured." Finally, you will consider how you may age.

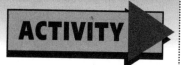

BEN: A STUDY IN GROWING OLDER

INTRODUCTION Ben was born in Russia in 1909, came to the United States when he was 3, and lived to be 87 years old. The following are four photographs of Ben during various stages of his life. Study them carefully and think about the following:

1. How did Ben's appearance change as he aged? What, if anything, remained the same?

2. If you had looked only at the first and last images, would you have been able to identify him as the same person? Explain your reasons.

3. You have seen Ben at age 3, 14, 35, and 75. Based on your knowledge from the module, during which of these time intervals do you think the most development occurred, physically and mentally? Explain your responses.

4. How do you think Ben might have felt as he looked back over his images as you have done?

5. As a young person somewhat removed from the process, what would you like to know about aging?

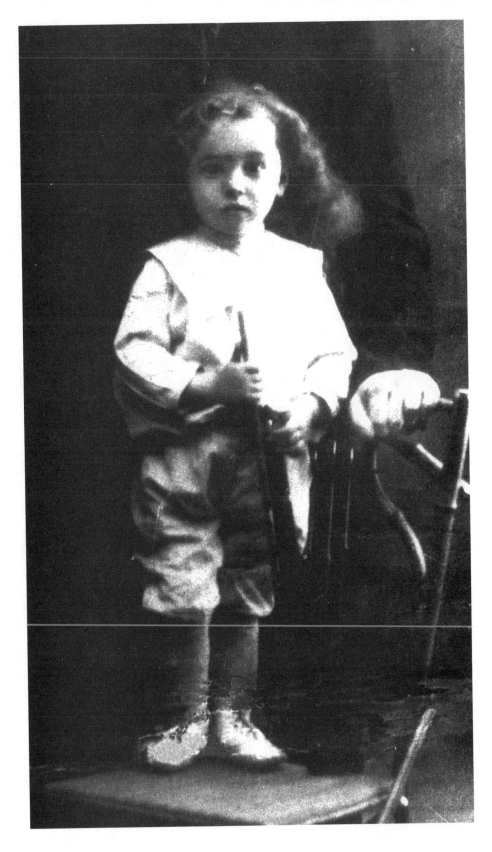

Figure 12.1
Ben at age 3.

Figure 12.2
Ben at age 14.

Figure 12.3
Ben at age 35.

Figure 12.4
Ben at age 75.

How Old Is Old?

How do we know if something or someone is old? We look at it and see physical characteristics that we associate with that object, that animal, or that person having been around a long time—rust, a broken slat, peeling paint, graying whiskers, wrinkled skin. In material things (inanimate objects) the ravages of time are often due to wear and tear, overuse and exposure to oxygen, pollutants, temperature, water, insects, and little children. The process of aging can be considered one more phase in the continuum of life, its features reflecting biological events that occur during this time. Aging may be viewed more commonly as the progressive loss of normal functions after sexual maturity that continues until the time of death. But the *causes* of aging in living organisms are not so easily identified.

OLD AS THE CELLS

Birthdays are one way to mark the passage of time, and a simple question of "How old are you today?" generally leads to a simple response: "8;" "15;" "25;" "39 again;" "none of your business;" "old enough to know better." These responses reflect either the passage of time chronologically or a societal perception of age. But how old are you really, biologically speaking? In reality, you may be only as old as your oldest cells, your nerve and muscle cells. These are the only kinds of cells that never divide or are replaced. During the juvenile and adolescent stages, they may increase in size (*hypertrophy*) but growth, defined as cell division, does not occur.

Many cells of your body, such as skin cells and blood cells, are dividing rapidly at your age. These new cells replace older cells which are sloughed off or otherwise discarded. When you are young, this is part of the growing process; cells are dividing rapidly, increasing the size of existing structures. During adulthood, growth no longer occurs, but older cells are continually being replaced by new cells. In old age, the balance shifts. The rate of replacement by newer cells slows down and does not keep up with the number of cells being removed; this accounts for some of the shrinkage seen in old age and the reduced capabilities for carrying out certain life functions.

While the nerve and muscle cells you have today are the same ones you were born with, most of your other cells are the descendants of your original cells. In reality, you are not the person you were five years ago. But you are definitely a close relative.

ONE AGES, THE OTHER DOESN'T

Almost all organisms grow and develop; but do all organisms age? Watching our beloved pets grow old and die, we can see that domesticated animals often survive to a ripe old age. Generally speaking, though, most animals living in the wild do not reach old age. In one way, old age may be an artificial state created by the interventions of humans.

Organisms living in predatory situations depend for survival on being in top physical form. After they reach sexual maturity many functions begin to weaken, possibly in part as a result of the slowdown in replacement of specialized cells. This can manifest itself in a number of ways: as loss of strength and stamina, decrease in height, hearing loss, decline in reproductive capacity (fertility), decline in the immune system, loss of bone mass, appearance of wrinkles. As systems begin to weaken in an individual, that individual's chances of surviving predation are diminished. Old age has become a luxury for those organisms whose lives are not fully dependent on physical fitness. As early humans became the hunter rather than the hunted, their life expectancy increased.

No longer required to run from things that ate them, humans could grow older. And as they grew older new enemies appeared. An immune system that no longer functions at peak means that diseases easily defeated in youth can become killers in old age. But as humans learn to conquer these diseases with drugs and vaccines, the less they rely on their immune system, and the older they may grow.

Does this mean eventual immortality? Maybe, maybe not. Many scientists believe that a time limit is built into our bodies, that people will die around the age of 100 even after humans have learned to cure every disease in existence. That is, people can die of old age after reaching their natural time limit. What about those reports of people living to the age of 160 as the result of clean living and eating yogurt? The accuracy of these reports is described in a cartoon by Sidney Harris in which one elderly villager explains to a young visitor, "Our reputation for longevity is based on several factors: hard work, simple food, lack of stress, and the inability to count correctly."

Is aging inevitable? Certain animals such as lobsters, turtles, alligators, and female flounders seem to age not at all or at a very slow rate. One thing these organisms have in common is that they are of indeterminate size. That is, unlike most organisms that have a predetermined size, such as mammals, birds, and many insects, these organisms keep growing and growing and growing, increasing in size indefinitely.

A striking example of the association of indeterminate growth with lack of aging is the flounder. The female grows indefinitely and does not show age changes, but the male reaches a fixed size and ages (see Figure 12.5). How this happens is a mystery. Does the ability to grow indefinitely mean that these animals can continually replace vital specialized cells and therefore can avoid the weakening and loss of functions associated with aging? Again, this is not known. These animals are not, however, immortal. They still succumb to the vicissitudes of disease, accident, and death by causes unknown.

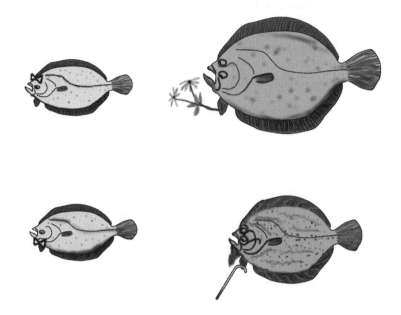

Figure 12.5
Female flounder continues to grow and never shows signs of aging; male flounder reaches a predetermined size and shows physical deterioration.

THEORIES OF AGING

So where do we organisms fated for a specific size and old age go "wrong"? What causes aging? Is it merely the inability of our cells to keep on dividing? If we found a way to keep on growing, would we live much longer, more youthful lives (although in the large economy-size version of ourselves)?

Throughout history, people have observed aging and developed many theories and explanations. An early theory of aging hypothesized that animals begin their lives with a limited amount of some vital substance. As this vital substance is consumed, age changes occur that eventually lead to a loss of vigor. When the vital substance is exhausted, death ensues. Variations in life expectancy among different organisms are explained by the difference in the amount of vital substance possessed by each animal at birth. To date, no evidence for this vital substance exists.

A modern day version of the vital substance theory was proposed by Leonard Hayflick in 1961, when he discovered cells possess their own biological clocks which determine a cell's ultimate life span. Hayflick determined that each cell can divide only a limited number of times. Taking cells from human connective tissues (fibroblast cells) he demonstrated that after 35 divisions the cells divided more slowly, and after the 50th division, stopped dividing altogether and died. He further showed that cells taken from young humans divided more times than cells taken from elderly humans and that fibroblasts taken from mice divided only 15 times before dying, a reflection of the shorter life span

(a)

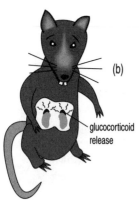

(b)

glucocorticoid release

(c)

R.I.P.

(d)

Figure 12.6
Glucocorticoids may be involved in the aging process: (a) a male marsupial mouse mates; (b) large amounts of glucocorticoid hormone are released and many metabolic processes shut down; (c) the mouse undergoes a rapid aging process; (d) the mouse dies.

of a mouse compared with a human. This theory of programmed senescence of cells suggests that the aging process is built into the genetic makeup of an organism and that aging is inevitable.

In 1882, a German biologist, August Weismann, proposed the "wear and tear" theory of aging. This theory suggested that aging occurs as organisms accumulate damage from the normal abuses of everyday life which, ultimately, erodes the normal biochemical activities that occur in cells, tissues, and organs.

A biochemical explanation of wear and tear might involve the formation of chemicals known as free radicals which can inflict damage on other molecules such as DNA and enzymes. Free radicals are formed as the result of normal metabolic processes; their accumulation, so the theory goes, can result in the changes associated with age.

While some organisms seem to age not at all or very slowly, others seem to age overnight and die in a flash. Pacific salmon and marsupial mice are examples of two organisms which exhibit an accelerated aging and death process. During mating season, salmon return upstream to the pools where they were born in order to spawn. A few days after spawning they die, en masse. Marsupial mice, native to Australia, have an annual, synchronized mating season after which, in the course of a few weeks, all the males die.

Studies over the past thirty years have traced this rapid aging and death to a sudden release of hormones known as *glucocorticoids.* Glucocorticoids are ordinarily secreted under stressful situations in which a lot of energy is required for responding to a physical or emotional emergency, such as an attack by a predator. Glucocorticoids work by freeing glucose from storage into the blood where it can be metabolized to form chemical energy. Glucocorticoids also turn off all kinds of long-term, energy-consumptive metabolic processes such as digestion, growth, reproduction, tissue repair, and the maintenance of the immune system.

What does this have to do with aging? Pacific salmon and marsupial mice age suddenly and die when their bodies release a flood of glucocorticoids. This release turns off many of the essential life functions, which is similar to what we observe as functions become impaired in the normal aging process. It has the apparent effect of almost instantly aging and killing these animals.

Certain persons undergoing physical and emotional stress have been said to have "aged overnight." Could rapid aging be an actual biological phenomenon brought on by a massive release of glucocorticoids in response to a stressful situation? Although stress may be a factor, most likely, aging is not the result of a single event or biochemical mechanism.

A rare hereditary disease called progeria, which afflicts children, is an example of accelerated aging in people. Progerics appear to experience accelerated aging by the age of twelve. Shortly before their deaths, they may have gray hair or be completely bald, have scratchy voices common to elderly people, and suffer from hearing loss, arteriosclerosis, or heart disease. However, progeric children are not aged in every respect. They do not show increased tendencies toward dementia or cancer—two major diseases linked to aging. Studies suggest that aging is the result of many different mechanisms that work together to cause senescence.

THE PICTURE OF YOUTH

The subject of Oscar Wilde's novel *Portrait of an Artist: The Picture of Dorian Gray* never aged. His secret was a self-portrait that aged for him. Humans have always sought ways to elude the ravages of time and to retain eternal youth. Perhaps the oldest written testament to these attempts is seen in an Egyptian papyrus from 1600 B.C. entitled "Book for Transforming an Old Man into a Youth of Twenty." It describes how to prepare an ointment for this purpose which, it says, has been "found effective myriad times." Taoist writings from sixth-century China held that eternal youth and immortality could be attained by keeping the body in harmony by balancing the two opposing principles of the body, the yin and the yang. Any imbalance in the forces results in illness and aging. These forces could be kept in balance through proper diet, exercise, good mental health, and by certain herbal remedies.

Myths and legends about the rejuvenating properties of water and food abound in many cultures. Even before Ponce de Leon and his quest for the fountain of youth, people in other cultures, such as Hindu, Greek, and Roman, claimed that mineral and thermal springs could cure illness and delay the aging process. Foods such as ambrosia of the Greeks, soma of the Hindu, and octli of ancient Peru and Mexico were also credited with these powers. In thirteenth-century England Roger Bacon, a scholar and alchemist, argued that life and youth could be extended by maintaining good health through diet, exercise, breathing, elimination, sexual activity, rest, and control of the emotions. In addition, Bacon maintained that secret potions, drinks, and foods—the elixirs of life—could be brewed and would extend youth and vitality indefinitely. However, the recipe for such elixirs eluded him and other alchemists of the day.

Are these waters, elixirs, and advice about healthful living so different from modern-day approaches to maintaining our youthful vitality? People are forever looking for ways to delay their destiny of decline—new diets for that bulging waistline, exercise machines for those sagging muscles, anti-wrinkle creams and cosmetic surgery for every square inch of flesh, antioxidants for those pesky free radicals, and the list goes on and on.

Reports that certain hormones, produced in youth but sadly lacking in the elderly, can reverse some aspects of the aging process bring hope to those who have no portrait to do their aging for them. Studies in which elderly men received injections of human growth hormone suggest that supplements of this hormone can increase muscle mass, cause loss of body fat, restore elasticity to skin, and increase energy. However, when the treatments were stopped, the youthful characteristics were lost.

Modern medicine and cosmetology may, in fact, be able to maintain that youthful appearance well into the golden years of many individuals, but will it ever slow the aging process and extend the human life span? That is not clear. Medicine has made great inroads into overcoming many major diseases—infectious diseases, heart disease, and certain kinds of cancer. But whether the aging process can ever be understood enough to be "cured" is open to speculation. Also open to debate is the desirability of such a goal. Would extending life create a whole series of ethical and biological dilemmas with which society is ill-equipped to cope? Is the delay or elimination of aging a high priority for research and development?

▶ ANALYSIS

Write responses to the following in your notebook.

1. How would you define "aging"?

2. Is aging a natural and inevitable process? Why or why not?

3. Describe the main changes that occur in aging organisms. Explain the biological basis of the changes, based on the theories of aging described in the reading.

4. What if biological research found a way to stop or slow down the aging process? In a short essay entitled "What If No One Aged?" discuss the social, economic, and ethical consequences if a treatment were available for preventing the aging process. Include the following in your essay:
    −   ways in which individuals who have lived a long time uniquely contribute to society
    −   a comparison of the social and economic consequences of a population with a large percentage of aging individuals to a population where people get older but do not age
    −   the social and economic consequences of a population in which no one dies
    −   the ethical issues that might result from the availability of such a treatment
    −   your opinion as to whether or not research to develop ways to prevent aging should be done and an explanation of your decision

THE POETRY OF AGING

The following poems are descriptions of different individuals' perspectives on growing old. As you read them, think about:
- how the aging process is represented in each poem
- what it seems to mean to the poet
- what it means to you

Then, imagine yourself in 50 years. Create your own poem, short story, essay, drawings, or any other expression to depict how you think you might feel physically and mentally and how life might have changed for you.

BODY
—Lillian Morrison

I have lived with it for years,
this big cat, developed an
affection for it. Though it is
aging now, I cannot abandon it
nor do I want to. I would love
to throw it about in play but
must be careful. It cannot sum-
mon that agile grace of old. Yet
it's really pleasant to be with,
familiar, faithful, complaining
a little, continually going about
its business, loving to lie down.

ATHLETE GROWING OLD
—Grace Butcher

The caution is creeping in:
the step is hesitant
from years of pain;
a soft grunt bends the body over,
and straightens it.
The skin loosens; everything moves
nearer the ground.

To overcome the softening,
the yearning towards warmth,
she exercises,
makes her muscles hard,
runs in the snow,
asks herself when she is afraid,
"What would you do now if
you were not afraid?"

She listens for the answer
and tries to be
like that person who speaks,
who lives just outside
all her boundaries
and constantly calls her
to come over, come over.

LIFE MUST GO ON
—Joanne Seltzer, excerpted from A Place for Mother

Your hair has turned white.
Your skin is parchment.
You have a bulldog's jowls.

You ask yourself
what Mother's face is doing
in the mirror.

She sticks out her tongue.

You wonder where the years went
and with horror
realize you forgot to flush
the toilet.

*"Body," "Athlete Growing Old," and "Life Must Go On" used with
permission by Lillian Morrison, Grace Butcher, and Joanne Seltzer, respectively,
from* When I Am An Old Woman I Shall Wear Purple, *Papier-Mache Press, 1987.*

BEAUTIFUL OLD AGE
—D. H. Lawrence

It ought to be lovely to be old
to be full of the peace that comes of experience
and wrinkled ripe fulfillment.

The wrinkled smile of completeness that follows a life
lived undaunted and unsoured with accepted lies.
If people lived without accepting lies
they would ripen like apples, and be scented like pippins
in their old age.

Soothing, old people should be, like apples
when one is tired of love.
Fragrant like yellowing leaves, and dim with the soft
stillness and satisfaction of autumn.
And a girl should say:
It must be wonderful to live and grow old.
Look at my mother, how rich and still she is!
And a young man should think: By Jove
my father has faced all weathers, but it's been a life!

"Beautiful Old Age" copyright 1971, from The Complete Poems of D. H.
Lawrence. *Used by permission of Viking Penguin, a division of Penguin Books
USA Inc.*

EXTENDING IDEAS

▶ Telomeres are long segments found at the ends of chromosomes that contain repeated sequences of DNA. The number of repeats found within telomeres of a particular cell may be indicative of how often that cell can divide. Whenever a cell divides it loses between five and twenty segments of its telomeres. If aging is a reflection of the number of times a cell can divide, could aging be delayed by increasing the number of telomeres in cells by genetic manipulation? Research current studies on telomeres and aging and discuss the implications of this work.

▶ Volunteer at a home for the elderly. Interview individuals to find out what their lives were like at your age.

▶ Examine newspapers, magazines, radio, and television for advertisements for products which promise some form of youth. Determine what these products claim to do, what aspects of aging they address, and how they validate their claims. Decide whether you are convinced or not of the advertisements' claims.

▶ Hospitals distinguish between "chronological" age which is determined by a person's birth date, and "biological" age which is determined by how well individuals do according to certain criteria and tests such as blood pressure, metabolic rate, lung capacity, response time, etc. For example, chronologically a person may be 50 years old, but "biologically" he or she may have the body of a 30-year-old. Contact your local hospital and find out the kind of tests they use to determine "biological" age and what you can do to keep your body fit as you grow older.

▶ Choose one theory about aging from the reading "How Old Is Old?" that you, as a researcher, might wish to pursue further. Describe:
   – which theory you chose;
   – why you find it intriguing;
   – one specific question about that theory you would like to pursue;
   – how you might investigate this theory; and
   – how this research might lead to a "treatment" for aging.

ON THE JOB

GERONTOLOGIST   Are you interested in working with or having a direct impact on the lives of older people? Gerontologists may either work directly with older people or work on their behalf.

Gerontology is the study of the physical, mental and social changes that occur during the aging process and in individuals as they grow from middle age through later life. Geriatrics is the study of health and disease in later life and the comprehensive health care of older persons. Gerontologists who work directly with older people may be involved in providing direct care in hospitals, nursing homes or through adult day care or home care programs. They might also develop activities and programs, counsel older people and their families about issues of caregiving, or advise clients about estate planning and investments, financing long-term care or housing options. Professionals who work on behalf of older people might conduct scientific research on the aging process and diseases associated with aging, analyze issues such as retirement opportunities, income maintenance, health care or housing. As the world's population ages, gerontologists are investigating societal changes that result from our aging population and its impact on policies and programs. Individuals interested in gerontology have several educational options. One way is to specialize in aging within another discipline such as anthropology, architecture, biology, or psychology. A second way is through continuing education that focuses on aging. A third way is through a degree program in gerontology which is offered at every post-high school level (a two year college degree, a four year college degree, or master's or doctoral degree). Gerontologists work in a variety of settings. Classes such as biology, psychology, and English are useful.

PRACTITIONER OF TRADITIONAL CHINESE MEDICINE   Would you like to help people utilize alternative approaches for maintaining good health? The philosophy of Chinese medicine embraces the belief that maintaining the balance within the body can prevent disease and stave off the ravages of the aging process. This balance can be attained by consuming healthful foods, achieving inner calm through exercise and meditation, and utilizing ancient practices of acupuncture and herbal remedies. The demand for alternative forms of medicine is increasing in the United States. Licensing of acupuncturists and herbalists occurs in many states and requires two to four years of training after college at an accredited school of acupuncture or oriental medicine and the passing of state boards in acupuncture and herbal medicine.

GLOSSARY OF TERMS

The following terms can be found on the listed page in the Student Manual unless otherwise noted. ◆ indicates pages which you may receive from your teacher.